A MODEL FOR MAKING
DISCIPLES

John Wesley's Class Meeting

D. MICHAEL HENDERSON

FRANCIS ASBURY PRESS
of Evangel Publishing House
Nappanee, Indiana 46550

Scripture quotations are from the *Holy Bible, King James Version*.

Cover design by Larry Stuart.

ISBN-10: 1-928915-70-1
ISBN-13: 978-1-928915-70-6

Library of Congress Card Number: 97-060624

Printed in the United States of America

8 7 6 5

This book is dedicated to my father,

William M. Henderson,

Who served as a Methodist pastor for more than fifty years. He has been my mentor and model in that same art of pastoral care which John Wesley learned from his father Samuel.

Preface

John Wesley has exerted a significant influence on my life, even though he lived two centuries before me. I was reared among an extended family of devout "Wesleyans": My father, my grandfather, and my uncles were all Methodist ministers who claimed John Wesley as their spiritual patriarch. I grew up thinking of myself as a "Wesleyan," probably more from the Wedgewood bust of Wesley that sat on our piano and the stern pictures of him that lined my father's study than from any understanding of his ideas or practices. My childhood years were enriched with countless stories about Wesley's life and frequent anecdotes about his ministry which were woven into my father's sermons. As I began to participate on my own in church leadership during my high school years—helping with the Methodist Youth Fellowship, speaking in country churches, working in youth camps—I began to read Wesleyan materials and developed a more personal loyalty to the tradition which bore his name.

The college which I attended, Asbury College, was founded to promote the doctrines associated with John Wesley. It had been named for Wesley's American representative, the Methodist bishop and circuit rider Francis Asbury. Here again, the theological emphases and their practical implications were impressed on my thinking, and my self-consciousness as a "Wesleyan" was further strengthened. Following college, I attended Asbury Theological Seminary—across the street from Asbury College in the tiny village of Wilmore, Kentucky, but no less Wesleyan in its concentration. It was here that I did my first serious papers on Wesleyan theology and history.

The next development in my identification with John Wesley was two-fold: I was appointed as senior pastor of a Methodist Church in West Haven, Connecticut, and at the same time I did further historical studies at Yale University. My research, although directed by a Lutheran, a Presbyterian, and a Congregationalist, centered on Wesley's theology, particularly his relationship to the Dutch theologian, Jacobus Arminius. It was fascinating to me to discover that Wesley had come to identify himself as an "Arminian" in much the same way that I had become a "Wesleyan": by birth, by childhood reinforcement, by practical experimentation, and finally by serious study and comparison with other schools of thought. I completed my thesis at Yale on Wesley's identification with the theology of Arminius, but in the process I discovered considerable data which was to lead me in new directions of research, away from the field of theology and more into the area of educational innovation. The data seemed to indicate that the effectiveness and uniqueness of both Wesley and Arminius (and Arminius's mentor, Peter Ramus) was as much due to their educational methods as it was to their theological formulations.

I decided to pursue a new course of research into the methods of Wesley's ministry and the principles of instruction which he seemed to employ so effectively. Opportunity to continue that line of study came in 1974 as I entered the graduate school of Indiana University in the field of adult education, with additional studies in religious studies and instructional systems technology. My courses provided me with new tools for evaluation of educational processes and new insights into the relationship between a particular educational philosophy and its methodological ramifications. My M.A. thesis again reflected my interest in Wesley, but this time with a focus on his instructional tools, particularly the class meeting. So, I attempted to show how Wesley had designed a usable group instrument, the class meeting, which was adopted by non-religious movements, in this case, the Chartists. That study provided much of the impetus for a wider dissertation project on Wesley's entire instructional system.

I am indebted to those who have fostered within me a deep attachment to Wesley and to the tradition which he established; I am equally grateful to those who have challenged and tempered my Wesleyanism; and I am most appreciative to my professors at

Asbury, Yale, and Indiana University who have given me the technical skills to research, evaluate, extract, and use the educational principles which John Wesley employed so effectively.

D. Michael Henderson, 1997

CONTENTS

Introduction

John Wesley created an instructional system which brought about a national spiritual renewal in eighteenth-century England. His techniques for nurturing and training Christian disciples not only brought personal transformation to tens of thousands of individual working-class believers, but a moral reformation to the nation as well. The movement Wesley spawned was derisively called "Methodism," because even his detractors recognized that the heart of the movement was a method—a powerful and effective educational method.

Wesley's unique "method" combined several interlocking group techniques to construct a ladder of personal spiritual improvement. All sincere Christians, whatever their intelligence or background, could work up that ladder simply by faithful participation, from one level of spiritual maturity to the next. The "rungs" on Wesley's ladder of Christian discipleship were small interactive groups—the class meeting, the band, the select band, the penitent band, and the society. Each group within the system was designed to accomplish a specific developmental purpose, and each group had its own carefully defined roles and procedures to ensure that the central objectives were accomplished.

The heart of this revolutionary system was a cell group of six to eight people which Wesley named "the class meeting." They met weekly to give an account of their personal spiritual growth, according to the rules and following the procedures which Wesley had carefully crafted. The class meeting proved to be such an effective tool for radical personal change that it can be acknowledged as the pivotal element of the Methodist movement, the vehicle of change, the medium which enabled the message to be internalized. The Methodist movement helped shape England's moral and spiritual destiny, and its impact continues to be felt around the world today through the institutions which bear its name. Of course, many factors contributed to the powerful effect which Methodism had on eighteenth-century society, both in England and later in America, but the key element was the class meeting.

Wesley set out to be neither a systematic theologian nor an educational reformer. He was an Anglican priest, a tutor at Oxford, an unsuccessful missionary to the American Indians, and a member of the renewal movement within the Church of England which became known as the Evangelical Awakening. He simply addressed the needs of those people who came under his spiritual supervision as best he could, incorporating and modifying existing pastoral methods into a workable synthesis.

Wesley wove the experiences of his own spiritual pilgrimage, his deep theological convictions, and the proven methods of other contemporary Christian leaders into a format which would address the needs of urban working-class people. The ingredients of his system of pastoral care were not unique. However, the final synthesis provided a dynamic tool for making Christian disciples which was effective in his day and useful in many other contexts.

Methodism enabled a large number of England's lower classes to cope with the social and spiritual chaos of the industrial revolution. The traumatic transition from a medieval and agrarian culture to a modern and industrial one was eased for the urban masses by the class meeting and its wider instructional system. Not only did vast hordes of urban laborers find personal salvation through the Methodist "method," but many historians believe that this same movement spared England from the kind of bloody revolution which ravaged other nations on the continent.

During the subsequent centuries, the institutions Wesley initiated have flourished and multiplied, reaching into most of the nations of the world with their organization and influence. In the United States alone there are more than twenty million Protestant Christians who trace their spiritual heritage back to this remarkable man. Historians have documented the impact of Wesley and Methodism upon the central values and directions of Western civilization and upon a significant branch of the Christian Church.

However, in both the subsequent development of Methodism and in the analysis of Wesley's contribution, the most critical element has nearly completely been neglected: the class meeting.

There are several compelling reasons to engage in a serious study of the class meeting now, more than two centuries after it was first practiced by the early Methodists. Even though its impact has been acknowledge by many authors, very little has been written about how Wesley developed the method, why it was so effective, and how its principles can be applied within other contexts. Perhaps this study will help reclaim for the Christian Church that dynamism which the class meeting restored to eighteen-century Anglicanism. Wesley certainly believed that these small groups recaptured the spiritual life of New Testament Christianity:

> Upon reflection, I could not but observe, this is the very thing which was from the beginning of Christianity. In the earliest times those who God had sent forth "preached the gospel to every creature." And of the αχροαται, "the body of hearers," were mostly either Jews or heathens. But as soon as any of these was so convinced of the truth, as to forsake sin and seek the gospel salvation, they immediately joined them together, and met these καταχουμενοι, "catechumens" (as they were then called), apart from the great congregation that they might instruct, rebuke, exhort, and pray with them, and for them, according to their inward necessities.[1]

The primary value in studying the class meeting today is to gain insights and methods for the Church's central task: making Christian disciples. Jesus commissioned his disciples to:

Go and make disciples of all nations, baptizing them in the name of the Father and of the Son and of the Holy Spirit, and teaching them to obey everything I have commanded you.[2]

He conferred upon those first apostles his authority to carry out that "Great Commission," and they accepted his assignment as their marching orders. They made disciples (as Jesus had commanded), and in the process Jesus built his Church (as he had promised), and that Church grew rapidly in strength and numbers.

However, as the Church continued to develop through the centuries, outside influences began to dilute and diminish its initial impetus. The tight focus on "making disciples" was lost, and many other activities gained priority. The task of maintaining Church institutions began to usurp the role that was originally assigned to making disciples, and the once-dynamic Christian movement began to fossilize from within.

From time to time, revival and renewal movements sprang up within the Church, breaking through the formality of rites and rituals to foster life and growth. Each wave of renewal was motivated by a desire to return to those principles and practices of the early Church which caused it to be so effective. The Wesleyan Movement of the eighteenth century was one of those attempts to rediscover the vitality of original Christianity. And, even today, there continue to be awakenings within the Church which are built around those same original themes.

The class meeting encapsulated several of the key principles of New Testament Christianity: personal growth within the context of an intimate fellowship, accountability for spiritual stewardship, "bearing one another's burdens," and "speaking the truth in love." It serves now as a model for those who have accepted the command of Jesus to make disciples. And, it provides useful insights about those processes by which Christian disciples learn to "do everything that I (Jesus) have commanded."

As the secular world has grown more sophisticated in its ability to gather and transmit information, the Church has co-opted many of its methods. Lifeless creeds have replaced the burning convictions which so characterized the early Church. Sterile meetings have taken the place of that intimate fellowship described in the New Testament. And the communication of inert information has supplanted the vital interaction entailed in the enterprise of "making disciples."

John Wesley was able to cut through the trappings of Anglicanism and recapture the spirit of *koinonia,* the supportive fellowship of primitive Christianity. Those who are committed to making disciples in the world of the twenty-first century will do well to learn from him the intricate workings of the class meeting and how those interactions fostered spiritual growth and serious discipleship.

A second arena in which this study can make a contribution is the field of educational innovation. The genius of Wesleyan revival was an instructional tool, more so than a theological distinctive or an organizational structure. The "method" which gave Methodism both its name and its overwhelming effectiveness was the class meeting. It was this "method" which gave Wesley and his associates the ability to give minute supervision to a vast army of growing Christians. As the architect of a well-disciplined movement, he was able to assimilate large population blocs into his organization in a short time, train them effectively in the rudiments of Christian discipleship, and mobilize them into an ardent corps of social change agents.

There is little precedent for the historical examination of instructional innovations. In the sophisticated sciences of "history of philosophy" or "history of theology," rational concepts have been examined as to their origins, applications, diffusion, influence, and transmission across cultures. An enormous literature supports the ongoing research into how various ideals and philosophies have shaped human progress. But this same intensity of systematic research has just begun to be applied to the world of innovation in communication and education.

Only recently have we begun to suspect that the medium of conceptual transmission may be as influential as the content of the message. The impact of the alphabet, the printing press, television, and the public school needs to be thoroughly examined and evaluated. It may be argued that the medium itself is the primary agent of change; that the ideas conveyed by that medium are less of a factor in the final outcome than the vehicle which conveyed them. And, it may be argued that the medium chosen to convey a given message determines not only the character of its reception but even shapes the quality of the message itself. For these reasons alone there is justification to investigate the origins of the class meeting and their effect on the process of making disciples. Is the medium in fact the message?

Finally, there is always value in adding to the store of knowledge about any historical event: in this case, the phenomenon know as the Evangelical Awakening or the Wesleyan Movement. Much of the material available for study on the instructional methods of that movement has been lost in dusty archives and forgotten collections of materials. Researchers will find worth in the accumulation of information about Wesley and his instructional system.

From those three directions, let us approach John Wesley's class meeting with the following questions:

1. What impact did this movement have upon England as a whole and specifically those working-class English people who joined it?
2. How did Wesley develop such an effective method?
3. What exactly was a "class meeting," and how did it fit into the wider system of Wesley's network of small groups?
4. What were the theological assumptions and underpinnings of his methodology? And finally,
5. How can the class meeting be a model for making disciples in the twenty-first century, or any century for that matter?

CHAPTER ONE

The Wesleyan Revolution

The eighteenth century was for England "the best of times; the worst of times." It was the beginning of the industrial revolution which whisked England out of the Middle Ages and into the modern industrial era. For those who owned the mills and factories during this economic boom, times were never better. They enjoyed all the luxuries and refinement of culture which their new-found wealth could buy. But beneath the belching smokestacks of their factories and in the smoky shadows of their grimy mills a vast horde of impoverished workers eked out a miserable living. The ever-widening gulf between the rich and the poor set in motion a powerful undercurrent that would have far-reaching implications for the future of the nation. Unbeknownst to the comfortable aristocracy, the seeds were already sown for a revolution.

That revolution did take place before the end of the century. The class system began to crumble, the poor gained the means to overcome their plight, and many of the social ills were corrected. In neighboring France, the revolution took the form of violent upheaval: The peasantry stormed the Bastille in 1789 and formed their own republic. In England the revolution was entirely opposite: It was quiet, orderly, and of a spiritual nature. It was led not by armed insurgents but by Anglican revivalists and their lay assistants. It was the Wesleyan Revolution.

John Wesley was a disillusioned young clergyman who returned to England in 1738 from an unsuccessful missionary trip to Georgia. His disappointment was not only in the venture to

America; he was mostly dissatisfied with his own spiritual condition. After several months of restless searching, Wesley found what he wanted: the assurance of God's pardon. Through the interaction of a small cell of fellow seekers, Wesley "found [his] heart strangely warmed." Accompanying his own spiritual rebirth came a compelling vision to reach the whole of England with the message of God's redemptive power. He chose as his goal: "to spread scriptural holiness throughout the land."

Wesley's vision was an audacious one because England in the mid-1700s was experiencing everything but holiness. The nation was awakening from its sleepy agricultural history and hurtling headlong into the Industrial Revolution. England had become the great seafaring nation of Europe, and with expanded trade the demand for manufactured goods had skyrocketed. The nation's center of activity shifted from the agricultural towns to the new manufacturing cities clustered near the coalfields, mostly in the north and west.

The landed aristocracy was quick to profit from this windfall in the trade and manufacturing. Factories and mills were built, ships were readied to carry the goods to foreign ports, and banking institutions sprang up to handle the surge of business transactions. Those who controlled the wealth rode a wave of unprecedented prosperity.

The poor, on the other hand, drifted in from the outlying agricultural areas, seeking work in the great cities. They became grist for the wheels of industry, cheap labor to run the mills and factories, much as twentieth-century villagers have crowded into the teeming cities of Latin America, Asia, and Africa. The countryside was drained of workers; the urban areas mushroomed with the incoming hordes of impoverished laborers. Uprooted from whatever cultural and family roots they had known before, they became easy prey for both the ruthless lords of industry and the moral vices of the urban slums.

The most tragic victims of the "wheels of industry" were the children of the working families. Many began at four or five years of age to work in the mines, the mills, and the brickyards. Lord

Shaftesbury, making a report to the House of Commons, reported children as young as three-and-a-half, half-clothed and malnourished, tottering under heavy loads of wet clay in the brickyards.[1] Less than one in twenty-five had any kind of schooling, and what formal education there was did more to teach a child to "mind his place in society" than to gain any useful skill.

One of the most demoralizing vices of the poor was widespread alcoholism, even among the children. In 1736 every sixth house in London was licensed as a grogshop. Gin consumption topped eleven million gallons a year in England alone. This epidemic of drunkenness eroded what little decency was left among the working people, leaving them adrift in hopeless despair. William Hogarth, popular British artist of the times, captured some of this degradation in his paintings, like the one entitled *Gin Land*.

Meanwhile, the rich were not only getting richer but settling into a comfortable and gracious style of living, completely oblivious to the plight of the poor in their mills and mines. For England, it was a time of colonial expansion, scientific discovery, cultural refinement, and economic growth. The art, literature, furniture, music, and theater of the time give the impression that English common sense had finally subdued the disorder and crudity which spoiled much of the rest of the world.

The Peace of Utrecht, which ended the War of the Spanish Succession in 1713, gave Britain the monopoly on slave trade. Wealthy planters returned from the North American colonies to spend their money in the more congenial homeland, bringing with them Negroes and Indians whom they sold again. Even English men and women were sold to ships going overseas, because the law allowed anyone in debt to be imprisoned or "indentured" to their creditors' companies. The reins of economic power were completely in the hands of the wealthy few. Beneath the sophisticated veneer of the governing classes, the English populace was gripped in a vise of poverty, disease, and moral decay.

Where was the Church in all this? Was there no redemptive ministry, no lifting of the burdens of the poor? Unfortunately, the

Church was in a sad state of deterioration. The Church of England catered almost exclusively to the upper strata of society. After the monarchy had been restored in 1660 and the austerity of Puritanism thrown off, the Church had drifted into a trifling worldliness. The clergy generally tended toward deism in theology and polite indulgence in lifestyle. Religion had lost any real impact in the daily lives of the people.

Dean Swift, popular author and social commentator, lamented,

> I suppose it will be granted that hardly one in a hundred among people of quality or gentry appears to act by any principle of religion; that great numbers of them do entirely discard it, and are ready to own their disbelief of all revelation in ordinary discourse. Nor is the case better among the vulgar, especially in the great towns.[2]

Churches were subsidized by the government, and pastors were paid "livings" from state tax revenues. Of the 11,000 "livings" in 1750, 6,000 were occupied by men who never set foot in their own parishes; they lived in London or on the continent and farmed their parishes out to the poorly-paid, under-trained curates. Very few paid any concern to their pastorates, especially in those districts from which the industrial workers came.[3]

Puritanism, once the bulwark of the working people, had reached its lowest point of influence in English life. Once a dynamic movement, its energies were now channelled into theological arguments and political wrangling. The masses of village folk who had once been the backbone of the Puritan Republic were now selling their religious birthright for factory jobs in the industrial cities. What remnants of Puritan piety they may have known were soon discarded in the moral confusion of the urban slums.

For close to a century the English aristocracy had legislated and pressured and coerced the general populace toward uniformity and regularity in religion, in reaction against the excesses of the Puritan commonwealth. The most dreaded malady of the religious establishment was what they termed "enthusiasm"—an epithet that connoted not only personal fanaticism but also that sinister mesmerism which was thought to excite the unstable masses toward anarchy and rebellion.[4] Religion had become so domesticated that only regularly ordained clergy, using approved liturgies, could conduct routine services within the territory they were assigned, and even then the services had to be conducted in facilities consecrated for that specific purpose. The consequence of all this standardization was not only that "enthusiasm" was quelled, but nearly every shred of spiritual vitality as well. English religion was dry as dust.

It was in this religious morass and cultural upheaval that John Wesley set about to "redeem the nation" and "spread scriptural holiness throughout the land." He was thirty-five years old, single, an ordained Anglican priest, and a sometime tutor at Oxford University. During his days at Oxford, he had established himself as a leader of a small group of zealous Christian students which was nicknamed the "Holy Club." His younger brother Charles was also a Holy Club member, as were several other bright young ministerial students.

At this point Wesley had a difficult choice to make: Would he aim at reformation of the nation from the top down, working among the intellectuals and the aristocracy to bring them back to their evangelical moorings? Or, would he take the message of holiness directly to the people, the countless hordes of England's illiterate and unchurched working class? That decision faces every new generation of Christian leaders and must be answered with renewed commitment with each successive effort toward awakening of the Church.

There had been some precedent for the first approach, although it had brought about no real turnaround for the English Church. Warburton and Butler had tried to counter deism and rationalism by brilliant philosophical argument, matching their opponents point by point with logical precision. Their efforts had been heroic, but the result was little more than the addition of dusty volumes to the sagging shelves of Oxford's theological library.

Wesley, as an instructor at Oxford, was in an ideal situation to follow that course, a course which in fact John Henry Newman would take at Oxford about a century later. But Wesley was disillusioned with the emptiness of "paper religion," especially that speculative theology laced with philosophy so popular at Oxford. He had parted ways with his old spiritual mentor, William Law, partly over Law's dabbling in philosophy and mixing it with religion. As Wesley said in a letter to Law: "So far as you add philosophy to religion, just so far you spoil it."[5]

Although this middle-aged scholar/priest was temperamentally drawn to the academic and cultural world of Oxford, he had a deeper conviction which would ultimately help determine his choice of audience. That conviction was his determination to recapture the spirit and methods of primitive Christianity. Jesus had not gathered his disciples from among the scribes and Pharisees; rather, he had called to himself rough fishermen and unlettered peasants from the hill country of Galilee. It was the common people who heard him gladly, not the intellectual elite. When the Apostle Paul set out to proclaim the gospel to the known world of the first century, it was to the despised Gentiles that he went. Nor were there any illustrations from the history of the church to indicate that mass movements begin from the top. If the nation of England were to be reformed according to any biblical pattern, it would have to begin with the workers, the miners, the rude peasants who were beyond the reach of the established church.

Actually, Wesley did not make this important decision—it was made for him by one of his former students and colleagues in the Oxford Holy Club, George Whitefield. Whitefield was a powerful young preacher (twenty-three at the time) who captivated large crowds in church services in London. In a day starved for any kind of public entertainment, his preaching both astonished and attracted vast congregations of Londoners. The largest churches in London, then a city of 600,000 people, could not contain the crowds of eager hearers, and thousands spilled out into the streets and adjoining courtyards.[6] Whitefield was the Billy Sunday of England; his bold denunciation of sin, fiery oratory, and impassioned calls for repentance made him a popular hero among the working people.

One of his later admirers, the American Benjamin Franklin, sized up his style this way:

> Every accent, every emphasis, every modulation of voice was so perfectly well-turned and well-placed, that, without being interested in the subject, one could not help being pleased with the discourse; a pleasure of much the same kind with that received from an excellent piece of musick.[7]

On one occasion, when Whitefield was preaching in America, Franklin devised an experiment to test Whitefield's speaking voice: He edged backwards through the crowd, away from the speaker, until he was at the farthest distance that Whitefield's diction could be distinguished easily. Then, using this distance as a base and counting the number of people within a given segment of the audience, Franklin calculated that Whitefield could easily address 30,000 people standing in an open place.[8]

Whitefield's popularity with the common people was a threat to the regular clergy. His spectacular style and his youthful exuberance soon earned him the reputation of an "enthusiast." When he took his preaching campaign to Bristol, the second largest city in England, he found the response even greater than in London. The crowds were larger and the opposition was stiffer. The excitement generated by the young evangelist was so contagious that the city fathers feared that rioting would break out among his followers.

The fears of the clergy were somewhat alleviated when Whitefield announced his intention to go to Georgia as a missionary, just as John and Charles Wesley had done (see chapter 2). At this time the colony was less than four years old, and the image of life in the jungles of North America was both frightening and romantic to the average Englishman. The crowds were sorry that he would be leaving, but the idea of a young man braving the wilds of Georgia to serve the Lord only further elevated their opinion of him. Whitefield was not only their Billy Sunday; now he was to become their Albert Schweitzer, nobly giving his talented life in service to the savages (both Indian and English) on the rugged American frontier.

His stay in America was short-lived, not because he was unsuccessful (as the Wesleys had been) but because he was consumed with a new mission. The frequent epidemics on the American frontier had left dozens of homeless orphans, so Whitefield set himself to the task of providing an orphanage for them. Faced with a shortage of funds, he recalled the enormous crowds which had packed the churches of London and Bristol to hear him preach. Surely they would help him build an orphanage! So he returned to England for a quick trip to enlist their financial support.

He arrived in England late in 1738 after a violently stormy nine-week passage. He anticipated that the churches would welcome him with open arms and give him an opportunity to promote his orphanage project. But during his absence an intense reaction to him had set in among the prominent pastors, so much so that many churches closed their doors to him. He continued to preach where he could, but the antagonism grew greater and greater.

During this time, the young evangelist received reports of a Welsh revival sparked by the outdoor preaching of an itinerant layman named Howell Harris.[9] On December 20, 1738, Whitefield established contact with Harris by letter,[10] since he was intrigued with the possibilities of reaching larger crowds of people than could jam into the inconvenient and increasingly inhospitable cathedrals. Harris's appeal had been to Welsh miners, a great bloc of the population which was normally beyond the reach of the established church. Whitefield also knew of just such an outcast society in England, and he began to make plans to reach the Kingswood coal-miners.

Kingswood was a cluster of dirty hamlets outside the city limits of Bristol, which itself was a notorious seaport city. Even though Bristol ranked in vice as England's eighteenth-century Corinth, it was not considered as vile as the Kingswood slums, which were the home of the coal-diggers in that area. The citizenry of Bristol, even the rugged sailors and slave traders, both despised and feared these coal-miners, who that same year had dug up and dismembered the corpse of a murderer because his suicide had robbed them the entertainment of a public execution.[11] Illiterate and impoverished and of a volatile temperament, they would occasionally go on a rampage through the city of Bristol, pillaging and destroying as they went searching for food. It was this group that Whitefield targeted as his congregation for outdoor preaching. Someone had said to him before his trip to Georgia, "Why go to America to preach to the redskins when we have savages enough among our Kingswood colliers?"[12]

The churches of Bristol offered him no encouragement. The clergy of the city had drifted so far from their orthodox moorings that Whitefield's presence was an offense and a threat. Shut out of the churches, he took his message to the infamous Newgate Prison, but soon even the jail was placed off limits to his sensational evangelism. The pastors of the large churches wanted no intrusion on their enjoyable, even luxurious, lifestyle. For example, the dean of one of the largest cathedrals in Bristol, Reverend Samuel Creswicke, was an avid sportsman who had little time for religious duties. His assistants carried on the churchly functions while he gave his attention primarily to cockfighting. He had constructed a cockpit beneath the dining room window of his rectory so that he and his guests could watch the cockfights as they dined.[13]

Unable to preach in the churches, or even in the prison, Whitefield made his first excursion into the Kingswood slums on February 17, 1739. He reported:

> I went up on a mount and spake to as many people as came to me. They were upwards to two hundred.[14]

He was so pleased with the outcome that he announced on that day that he would return the following Wednesday. That evening he wrote in his journal:

> Blessed be God! I have now broken the ice! I believe I
> was never more acceptable to my Master than when I
> was standing to teach those hearers in the open fields.
> Some may censure me, but if I thus please men I should
> not be servant of Christ.[15]

When he arrived the following Wednesday for his second service among the miners, such excitement had spread among the hovels that over two thousand gathered for the occasion. They stood quietly and reverently as the young preacher expounded his text.

During the next few weeks, Whitefield extended his open-air mission to public sites all around the Bristol area: churchyards, marketplaces, fields, brickyards, coal pits, even a bowling green. Thousands jammed the markets to hear him, and when he preached in the countryside, even the wealthy came out from Bristol in coaches and on horseback to hear his heart-stirring appeals. The uncouth coal-diggers at Kingswood had come under the spell of his powerful preaching, and as many as twenty thousand at a time would leave their squalid huts for a service in the open fields.

Whitefield described their hearty response:

> Having no righteousness of their own to renounce, they
> were glad to hear of a Jesus who was a friend of publi-
> cans, and came not to call the righteous, but sinners to
> repentance. The first discovery of their being affected
> was to see the white gutters made by their tears which
> plentifully fell down their black cheeks, as they came out
> of their coal pits. Hundreds and hundreds of them were
> soon brought under deep convictions, which, as the
> event proved, happily ended in a sound and thorough
> conversion. The change was visible to all, though num-
> bers chose to impute it to anything, rather than the fin-
> ger of God.[16]

Not only had Whitefield given evangelistic appeals; he had also been enlisting financial support for the orphanage in Georgia. As he made plans to return to America, he began to look for a successor in this innovative field-preaching ministry. The man to whom he turned was his Oxford colleague, eleven years his senior: John Wesley.

Whitefield took it for granted that Wesley would accept his invitation, and he even went so far as to fund an announcement in the Bristol newspaper to that effect.[17] However, in spite of the effervescent enthusiasm of his younger colleague, Wesley struggled with the decision. He held very strongly to his Anglican tradition about church order, and he especially distrusted any technique which could lead to anarchy or mob disorder. On the other hand, he had been stirred by the accounts of popular awakenings in New England under the leadership of Jonathan Edwards,[18] and he saw in the Bristol campaign the opportunity for such a reformation in older England. Unable to make a decision, he cast lots—an unlikely way, it seems, to make such a significant choice—but the lot said "Bristol" and the revolution that was to shake the nation made some small but important steps forward.

In his journal, he recorded the fears, which still lingered:

Sat. 31 March. In the evening I reached Bristol, and met Mr. Whitefield there. I could scarcely reconcile myself at first to this strange new way of preaching in the fields, of which he set me an example on Sunday; having been all my life (till very recently) so tenacious of every point relating to decency and order, that I should have thought the saving of souls almost a sin if it had not been done in a church.[19]

The next morning Whitefield took Wesley with him as he preached his final message in the Kingswood area. The effect on the people was so great that even the worst of Wesley's fears gave way to excitement about field preaching. The technique itself was revolutionary (by British standards), but it was only the beginning of the spiritual revolution which would transform English society during the next hundred years. That afternoon, in a brickyard, Wesley preached his first outdoor sermon:

> At four in the afternoon, I submitted to be more vile, and proclaimed in the highways the glad tidings of salvation, speaking from a little eminence in the ground adjoining to the city to about three thousand people. The Scripture on which I spoke was this... "The Spirit of the Lord is upon me, because He hath anointed me to preach the gospel to the poor. He hath sent me to heal the broken-hearted; to preach deliverance to the captives and recovery of sight to the blind; to set at liberty them that are bruised, to proclaim the acceptable year of the Lord.[20]

Whitefield had initiated and popularized mass evangelism to the unchurched, but Wesley organized the movement and brought it under systematic management. Whitefield hoped that those who had been "awakened" would follow through on their own initiative; Wesley left nothing to chance. He made sure that those who were serious about leading a new life were channelled into small groups for growth in discipleship. These little meetings were later called "classes" and formed the backbone of the Methodist reformation for the next century. The "class meeting" turned out to be the primary means of bringing millions of England's most desperate people into the liberating discipline of Christian faith.

In city after city, Wesley and his associates preached and organized people into class meetings for spiritual growth. Other contemporary reformers looked upon these decadent neighborhoods and threw up their hands in despair. It seemed hopeless that the plight of the poor could be remedied. Wesley looked at the same miserable conditions and saw a situation which was ripe for evangelism. Instead of abhorring their miseries and vices from a comfortable and safe distance, he eagerly sought the foulest circumstances in which to work. One of the most characteristic examples of his optimistic approach to odious situations is his description of his entry into the slums of Newcastle, the notorious "den of iniquity":

> We came to Newcastle about six, and, after a short refreshment, walked into the town. I was surprised: so much drunkenness, cursing, and swearing (even from the mouths of little children) do I never remember to have seen and heard before, in so small a compass of time. Surely this place is ripe for Him who "came not to call the righteous, but sinners to repentance."

> At seven I walked down to Sandgate, the poorest and most contemptible part of the town, and, standing at the end of the street with John Taylor, began to sing the hundredth Psalm. Three or four people came out to see what was the matter, who soon increased to four or five hundred. I suppose there might be twelve to fifteen hundred before I had done preaching....[21]

Using the powerful combination of field preaching and class meetings, the Methodist revival was underway. What happened as a consequence is still a matter of historical analysis. However, the nation was shaken to its foundations by a spiritual awakening. Early in the nineteenth century, historians began to weigh the effect Methodism had on the course of England's destiny. Wesley was acknowledged to be the guiding spirit of the age, much as Voltaire had been during the same period in France. French historian Elie Halevy popularized the thesis that the Wesleyan movement spared England the kind of bloody revolution which France had experienced. Other historians lined themselves up on either side of the "Halevy thesis," but generally agreed that the transformation of English society was largely due to the impact of Wesley and the movement he spawned.[22]

If, then, this movement was so significant, and if George Whitefield was its first and most popular spokesman, why then is it known as the Wesleyan Revival rather than the Whitefield Revival?

That question is crucial, not only to a historical understanding but also to a broader perspective on spiritual revolutions. Perhaps it is best explained by Adam Clarke, an early historian of Methodism, who quotes Whitefield himself on the issue:

> It was by this means [the formation of small groups] that we have been enabled to establish permanent and holy churches over the world. Mr. Wesley saw the necessity of this from the beginning. Mr. Whitefield, when he separated from Mr. Wesley, did not follow it. What was the consequence? The fruit of Mr. Whitefield's labors died with himself: Mr. Wesley's fruit remains, grows, increases, and multiplies exceedingly. Did Mr. Whitefield see his error? He did, but not till it was too late. His people, long unused to it, would not come under this discipline. Have I authority to say so? I have and you shall have it.

> Forty years ago I travelled in Bradford, the Wilts Circuit, with Mr. John Pool. Himself told me the following anecdote. Mr. Pool was well known to Mr. Whitefield, and having met him one day, Whitefield accosted him in the following manner:

> "Well, John, art thou still a Wesleyan?"

> Pool replied, "Yes, sir, and I thank God that I have the privilege of being in connection with him, and one of his preachers."

> "John," said Whitefield, "thou art in the right place. My Brother Wesley acted wisely—the souls that were awakened under his ministry he joined in class, and thus preserved the fruits of his labor. This I neglected, and my people are a rope of sand."[23]

The Wesleyan revolution is an illustration that long-lasting spiritual transformation is not the product of dynamic preaching or of correct doctrine. It comes only through serious disciple-building, in keeping with Christ's Great Commission to "go into all the world and make disciples." The class meeting which Wesley developed was the instrument by which preaching and doctrine were harnessed into spiritual renewal. It carried the revolution.

CHAPTER TWO

The Formation of Wesley's Method

John Wesley's life spans nearly the entire eighteenth century (1703-1791). By 1742, the general format of his educational framework was complete, except for minor alterations. However, that methodology emerged neither automatically nor instantaneously. The components had been assimilated one by one into a unified and cohesive system. His pragmatic approach led him to borrow and adapt ideas from a wide range of diverse models. The final product was not just a jumble of dissociated fragments but a refined synthesis of proven techniques.

Dr. Martin Schmidt has produced a helpful sketch of Wesley's life which he entitled *John Wesley: A Theological Biography.*[1] In this theological approach to personal history, he recasts the progress of Wesley's life in terms of the formation of his theology. Following Dr. Schmidt's precedent, let us look at Wesley's development as an educational innovator, tracing the elements of his method to the influential factors in his life. In Wesley's case, he was kind enough to future researchers to provide considerable evidence and reflection on the major forces which shaped his thinking. He kept record of the authors he read, what he thought of them, and which of their ideas he could utilize. He observed various models of group instruction, evaluated them, and left descriptive accounts of their adaptation into Methodism. What follows, then, is an attempt to thread together those factors into a chronological and biographical account.

A REMARKABLE BEGINNING

Much of Wesley's success as an educator can be traced to factors in his own training at home. The principles of learning which were instilled by his parents eventually constituted the backbone of his own educational philosophy. In later years, when John and his brother Charles had the opportunity to instruct thousands of people in personal spiritual growth, they employed many of the same methods their parents had used.

The home into which John was born provided much of the impetus for his later educational interests. His father Samuel was an Anglican clergyman and a biblical scholar of considerable renown.[2] Brilliant and erudite, although somewhat eccentric, the elder Wesley provided a lofty model of Christian scholarship for young John. He instructed his children in the rudiments of liberal education and classical languages, so that several of the children could read the Greek New Testament before the age of ten.[3] The crowning glory of his career was a ponderous *Commentary on the Book of Job*, the painstaking production of which probably had a more lasting impact on his sons than on the reading public. Charles Gildon, a contemporary of Samuel Wesley, affirmed that:

> He was a man of profound knowledge, not only of the Holy Scriptures, of the councils, and of the Fathers, but also of every other art that comes within those called liberal. His zeal and ability in giving spiritual direction were great. With invincible power he confirmed the wavering, and confuted heretics. Beneath the genial warmth of his wit the most barren subject became fertile and divertive.[4]

Such a breadth and intensity of knowledge alone must have been an inspiring and motivating factor to the youngsters in the Wesley home![5]

Despite Samuel's literary ability, he was a poor hand at practical affairs, and he displayed an overly argumentative temperament. His mismanagement and hotheadedness landed him in debtor's prison for at least a few months and in continual controversy throughout his life. No doubt his lifetime assignment to the dismal village parish of Epworth in the fen country of Lincolnshire had something to do with his lack of tact. Even there, in that remote district, angry villagers twice burned his house and often stabbed his cattle in efforts to silence his outspoken opinions. Within his own house he also felt the repercussions of his volatile temper. Once, when his wife refused to say "Amen" to his prayer for the king, he demanded an explanation. After she explained that she would not acknowledge William of Orange to be the rightful heir to the throne, Samuel declared: "If that be the case, you and I must part; for if we have two kings, we must have two beds."[6] He immediately departed for London, where he stayed several months. King William, the source of their disagreement, died that year (1702), and Samuel returned to Epworth. Less than a year later, in June, 1703, John Wesley was born, the child of their reconciliation.

John's mother, Susanna Wesley, was the daughter of a Nonconformist minister, Dr. Annesley, and she has been hailed by many as the epitome of Puritan domestic management: disciplined, methodical, and graciously austere.[7] She bore nineteen children, eight of whom died in infancy. Susanna was no stranger to a crowded household, since she was the twenty-fifth (and last) child of Dr. Annesley. Her father was a prominent London pastor and close friend of the Puritan leader Richard Baxter. However, despite her upbringing in this stronghold of Dissent, at age twelve she decided to become an Anglican, stating her reasons in a lengthy theological treatise.[8]

One key tenet of Methodism is clearly evident in the educational philosophy of Susanna Wesley: the management of the human will. Mrs. Wesley considered the mastery of the child's will to be the decisive factor in character-molding. She was willing to postpone the instruction of the mind, since that process demanded time; but the subduing of the will must be done right away. She felt that the major problems of intellectual learning would be avoided if the children first learned to respect and obey their parents. As the children grew up, she was quite lenient with their pranks and childish errors but very stern with rebellion, stubbornness, and deliberate disobedience of explicit rules.

This emphasis on the subjection of the will came to the Wesley household largely through popular devotional writings. Susanna was deeply impressed by the writings of the Catholic mystic Lorenzo Scupoli,[9] the Puritan Richard Baxter, and the Scottish Episcopalian Henry Scougal. She gleaned from their spiritual writings practical suggestions for family discipline and the cultivation of inward piety.[10] She came to consider self-will as the root of all sin and misery, and so she taught her children that the essence of Christianity was doing God's will rather than their own. If self-will could not be conquered, she reasoned, then the child would never be free to accomplish constructive good.

In her explanation of the need for mastering the will of the child, she includes the following paragraphs:

> I insist upon conquering the will of children betimes, because this is the only strong and rational foundation of a religious education, without which both precept and example will be ineffectual. But when this is thoroughly done, then a child is capable of being governed by the reason and piety of its parents, till its own understanding comes to maturity, and the principles of religion have taken root in the mind.

> I cannot yet dismiss this subject. As self-will is the root of all sin and misery, so whatever cherishes this in children insures their after-wretchedness and irreligion; whatever checks and mortifies it promotes their future happiness and piety. This is still more evident if we further consider that religion is nothing else than the doing the will of God, and not our own; that, the one grand impediment to our temporal and eternal happiness being this self-will, no indulgences of it can be trivial, no denial unprofitable. Heaven or hell depends on this alone. So that the parent who studies to subdue it in his

child works together with God in the renewing and saving a soul. The parent who indulges it does the devil's
work, makes religion impracticable, salvation unattain-
able; and does all that in him lies to damn his child, soul
and body, forever.[11]

This emphasis on personal discipline and spiritual submis-
sion became an essential component of John Wesley's educational
strategy as he applied it, not to children, but to the urban masses
who crowded into England's industrial centers. The principles of
moral development that were applied in the parsonage at Epworth
proved to be just as effective in shaping the lives of the coal miners
at Bristol. As one observer described Methodism, "It came in, not
to supplant any existing system of actual discipline, but to establish
a culture of some sort upon the vast, howling wilderness of popular irreligion."[12]

Another major theme in the Wesley home was the Puritan
zeal for the "care and cure of souls." Following the example of
Richard Baxter and other pastors, the Wesleys concentrated their
energies on encouraging personal spiritual growth in themselves
and others. Samuel pursued this theme in the cultivation of his
parish; Susanna implemented it in her home. She shared the strong
Puritan ideal of her father,[13] who visualized the family as "a little
gathered Church, where prayer, Bible-reading, catechizing, and
detailed personal instruction in the Christian faith provided a
framework for the whole shared life of the home."[14] With Samuel's
assistance in language study, Susanna conducted a school for her
children, giving them an excellent beginning in the rudiments of
formal schooling.

In addition to her tutorial duties with her large family, she
devoted an hour every week with each child to attend to his or her
spiritual progress. She considered the nurture of each child's religious life as a serious duty entrusted to her by God, and the highest calling an individual could receive. Each evening she took one
or two children aside alone to discuss religious questions and to
evaluate their spiritual improvement. These sessions were not for-

mal and stuffy, but warm and intimate sharing concerning the reality of God and the greatness of his provision and the joys of the Christian life. John's turn came on Thursdays. Far from resenting this minute inspection of his inner development, he welcomed each week's inquiry. Years later, while he was a student at Oxford, he fondly recalled these intimate times of spiritual conversation which he had shared with his mother.[15] In fact, he was able to remember many of those talks well enough to quote the major topics. Here again, a major concept was generated in Wesley's childhood that would motivate his work as an adult. Part of the genius of the Methodist movement was its concentration on individuals and their particular needs. Just as Susanna had tailored her spiritual instruction to the needs and interest of each child, so John and his associates individualized the tutoring of every person entrusted to their care.

Mrs. Wesley was also an innovator in community education. Once, during a period when her husband was away, she established a school in her kitchen for servants and children who had no other opportunity for instruction. The classes grew until they were drawing more than two hundred participants each week by the time Reverend Wesley returned.[16] At first he was shocked by this radical departure from accepted English behavior, but soon took leadership of the group himself. Probably unaware of the impact these kitchen classes were having on their own children, the Wesley parents modeled a revolutionary role which their offspring would carry to the fields and marketplaces of eighteenth-century England.

Although John Wesley was the founder of Methodism, Susanna Wesley gave Methodism its methodical nature. She sought to bring every activity, word, and even thoughts and motives into a well-regulated regimen. She passed on to her children the discipline of strict time management and orderly conduct. From infancy each child was trained to live on a regular schedule. Eating, sleeping, studying, praying, and recreation each had an appointed time and place. Lessons were from nine o'clock to twelve and from two to five daily with no interruptions. Family prayers were held at six p.m. followed by supper. At 7:00 the maid began to wash all the children so that by 8:00 all were in bed. Before the age of one year each child was so disciplined that if he must cry, he would cry softly.[17] Even when her sons went off to college, she persistently encouraged them to "methodize" their lives, evidenced by this letter of admonition to her son, Samuel Jr.:

> First, I would advise you, as much as is possible in your present circumstances, to throw all your business in a certain method, by which means you'll learn to improve every precious moment, and find an unspeakable facility in the performance of your respective duties. Begin and end the day with him who is the Alpha and Omega; and though my ignorance of the orders of your school makes it impossible for me to assign what time you should spend in private devotions, yet I'm sure if you do really experience what it is to love God, you'll redeem all the time you can for his more immediate service. What is in your own power you may dispose of, nor are your rules so strict as not to admit of some diversions. I'll tell you what rule I used to observe when I was in my Father's house, and perhaps had as little, if not less, liberty than you have now. I used to allow myself as much time for recreation as I spent in private devotion. Not that I always spent so much, but so far I gave myself leave to go, but no further. So likewise in all things else, appoint so much time for sleep, eating, company, etc....[18]

This fascinating home wove together some of the most powerful strands of educational thought then current in English life. Young John and Charles Wesley were absorbing instructional techniques that would serve them well in their coming struggles to enlighten the poor, the imprisoned, the alienated, the oppressed. Their learning environment was not at first the university classroom, but the kitchen hearth; their mentors were godly parents who viewed their offspring as sacred trusts. One of the most succinct summaries of the disparate influences which converged in the Wesley home is that of Martin Schmidt, who said,

> John Wesley was born into this remarkable household on 17th June, 1703. It brought together the heritage of Puritanism, Anglican churchmanship, and that concern for the care of souls, social activity and missionary zeal, derived from the revival of the Religious Societies. At the same time it drew its sustenance from Puritan culture of family life and from the nurture of individual souls found in Romantic mysticism. To this was joined the Halle type of pietism. Finally a place was given to liberal scholarship, and the harmonious, mystical piety of a Henry Scougal was held in high esteem. To all this was added Susanna Wesley's personal gift as a teacher. Although this was charismatic in the deepest sense of the word, it was nevertheless most methodically cultivated and practiced. Through this rich polyphony one leading theme resounds like a *cantus firmus*: it is that of the love of God which empowers man towards perfection. It might be said that here, in the cradle, the main content of John Wesley's thought was already being proclaimed.[19]

ORDINATION AND ORDERED LIFE

Wesley's formal schooling took place at Charterhouse[20] (a private boarding school) and Oxford. He received his bachelor's degree in 1724 at the age of 21 after five years of competent study, social adjustment, and at least nominal religious observance. He demonstrated considerable proficiency in classical studies, but his greatest delight was logic and debate.[21]

Then in 1724, the young graduate made a decision which would ultimately determine his mission in life. His father encouraged him to seek ordination in the Church of England and to dedicate his life to the priesthood. With an awareness of the towering examples of his forebears in the ministry, young John began to examine his life to determine whether he could attain to such a high calling. The entire tone of his life took on a new seriousness. He recalls,

> 4. When I was about twenty-two, my father pressed me to enter into Holy Orders. At the same time, the providence of God directing me to Kempis's *Christian Pattern*, I began to see that true religion was seated in the heart and that God's law extended to all our thoughts as well as words and actions.... I began to alter the whole form of my conversation, and to set in earnest upon "a new life." I set apart an hour or two a day for religious retirement. I communicated every week. I watched against all sin, whether in word or deed. I began to aim at, and pray for, inward holiness.

> 5. Removing soon after to another college, I executed a resolution which I was before convinced was of the utmost importance—shaking off at once all my trifling acquaintance. I began to see more and more the value of time. I applied myself closer to study. I watched more carefully against actual sins; I advised others to be more religious, according to the scheme of religion by which I modeled my own life.[22]

John's father Samuel advised him to undertake a stiff course of technical theology with special emphasis on the study of biblical languages and the scholarly equipment which a clergyman might need. Susanna, reflecting her deeply-ingrained Puritan training, urged him to give his primary attention to practical experiential divinity, that pastoral devotion in which the Puritan ministers excelled.[23] Accordingly, John did both. But, as it turned out, the devotional writers provided him with the behavior-shaping tools of both his personal life and his public methodology. Even in his later years, he maintained that the formative influences in the forging of his distinctive lifestyle were found in four books: Thomas a Kempis's *Imitation of Christ*, Jeremy Taylor's *Holy Living and Dying*, and William Law's *Christian Perfection* and *A Serious Call to a Devout and Holy Life*.[24] Each of these authors outlined rigorous and detailed schemes of ascetic discipline geared to maximize Christian devotion. Wesley fashioned a schedule for himself based on the suggestions of these writers and set about reordering his existence. He wrote to his mother: "Leisure and I have taken leave of one another."[25]

Wesley's "conversion" to a life of intense discipline marks the first plateau of self-actualization in his spiritual and educational pilgrimage. From this time on, every endeavor would bear the indelible stamp of this experience. The preoccupation with the prudent use of each day would become one of the hallmarks of Methodism. The accountability to a set of predetermined guidelines would distinguish every enterprise which bore the Wesleyan name. Above all else, Methodism was to become a method; a strenuous, meticulous, disciplined method.

THE HOLY CLUB

John Wesley was called back to Oxford as a tutor in 1729. As Fellow of Lincoln College, he had been appointed to supervise and tutor a group of undergraduates in both their academic and spiritual progress.[26] At that time, three undergraduates from different colleges had been meeting four nights weekly for study of the classics and reading from the Greek New Testament. One of the members was Charles Wesley, John's younger brother.[27]

John quickly assumed leadership of the study group and gave it a more disciplined direction. The younger students readily responded to his suggestions for better ways to organize their time, so that the regimen of the group soon resembled John's own ascetic lifestyle. To classical studies and Bible reading were added regular periods of prayer, fasting, confession, and frequent partaking of the sacrament. In addition, the students began to search out opportunities for service and witness in the poorer sections of the city. They visited the sick, elderly, and imprisoned, and provided clothing and financial aid where they could. Their disciplined manner attracted the scorn of their fellow students, and they were dubbed "The Holy Club," "The Bible Moths," or "The Methodists," the name which Wesley's followers bear to this day.[28]

Although the Oxford Holy Club drew considerable attention, it was not unique in eighteenth-century Anglican practice. A half-century earlier Dr. Anton Horneck and others had originated the Religious Societies, voluntary associations of young men for the pursuit of a distinctively Christian way of life.[29] The prescription of the Societies was informal discussions on spiritual topics plus guidelines for daily conduct closely related to the prayers and ordinances of the Church of England. The rise of this movement, along with the Society for the Propagation of the Gospel (S.P.G.) and the Society for the Promotion of Christian Knowledge (S.P.C.K.), illustrated the fact that new spiritual vitality demanded more flexible organizational modes than were presently allowed in the Anglican framework.[30] The fossilization of established church structures pushed these more dynamic forces into voluntary, semi-independent factions on the fringes of church life. The ardor cultivated in the Religious Societies played a major role in both the Evangelical Awakening in England under the Wesleys and the Welsh Revival under the leadership of Howell Harris.[31]

The Holy Club owed much of its structure to the Religious Societies model. Samuel Wesley, John's father, had been a great admirer of this movement and had published an encouraging letter to them in 1699. The Holy Club members themselves were frequent participants in meetings of the Societies.[32]

In the spiritual exercises of the Holy Club, John Wesley's instructional technique was taking shape. Much like the Religious Societies' program, biblical principles were discussed and their implications examined in the context of a small supportive group. But Wesley added a new dimension. Rather than allow the process to end with cognitive acquisition, he demanded practical performance.[33] Once the personal implications of a concept under study were clear, the Holy Club members mapped a strategy for a real-life experiment. As their practice of it progressed, they evaluated their performance and reinforced successful execution of it. Not content to be "hearers only," they determined to be "doers of the Word."[34] Educational theorists had not yet formulated the notion of performance-based objectives, but Wesley was doing exactly that. Although his approach to group learning still had considerable refinement to undergo, he was employing the interpersonal dynamics of an intimate group to facilitate behavioral change. The Holy Club became a functional model for other group experiments.

THE MISSION TO AMERICA

In 1735 Wesley accepted the chaplaincy of General Oglethorpe's colony in Georgia. The original plan entailed missionary work among the Indians, but this was soon abandoned, and John became pastor of the English churches at Savannah and Frederica.[35]

During his thirty-month stay in the New World, he was able to try out his group learning model, fashioned after the Holy Club, on an entirely different population. The coarse settlers on the American frontier were a far cry from the sophisticated Oxford set. However, the diminutive priest soon had the entire congregations divided into smaller groups. These met regularly for exhortation, instruction, and correction. From these initial groups, Wesley chose a small number of "faithful men" with whom he met with on Sunday afternoons for more intensive training. He records the occasion in his journal for April, 1736, thus:

> Not finding as yet any door open for the pursuing our main design (ministering to the Indians), we considered in what manner we might be most useful to the little flock at Savannah. And we agreed (1) to advise the more serious among them to form themselves into a sort of little society, and to meet once or twice a week, in order to reprove, instruct, and exhort one another. (2) To select out of these a smaller number for a more intimate union with each other which might be forwarded, partly by our conversing singly with each, and partly by invit-

ing them all together to our house: and this, accordingly, we determined to do every Sunday in the afternoon.[36]

The establishment of two levels of participation marked the initiation of a key factor in the Methodist movement: a hierarchy of instructional groupings based on readiness of the learner and faithfulness at a lower level. Every parishioner was expected to participate on at least a minimal level, but provision was made for those who aspired to greater involvement. At this time there were only two levels; as Wesley's ministry expanded, more levels would be added.

The American application of the Holy Club model brought several significant changes in Wesley's approach to the training of Christian disciples. The first had to do with the relation of the discipleship groups to the church. At Oxford, the Holy Club had existed as a separate and supplementary agency, much like the Religious Societies. But, in marked contrast to the Societies, Wesley's groups in Georgia were not voluntary agencies which existed alongside the church.[37] Rather, they were divisions of the congregation. The Religious Societies had extracted only those young men, usually single, who were eager to strive for spiritual maturity. As they increased in both knowledge and zeal, there naturally arose a great disparity between their experience and that of the rest of the congregation. To Wesley's thinking, Christian growth was normative for every member of the congregation, not just a zealous elite. Therefore, Wesley was not creating another organization, but simply deepening the existing one. This expectation that every member would participate aroused some serious educational problems. Basically there were two difficulties: how to get everyone involved, and how to arrange instruction to match various levels of intelligence, experience, and motivation. One evidence of Wesley's genius is that he *did* discover solutions to these perennial bottlenecks to the group instruction process.

A second shift concerned the nature of the Christian mission and the status of the missionary. In the terminology of traditional educational institutions, this is the age-old dilemma of how the teacher visualizes his role toward his students. During his childhood, Wesley had been exposed to two basic models of missionary service.[38] One was that of the German pietists, mainly of the Danish-Halle strain. Their concept of the role of missionaries was that of foreign religious entrepreneurs, independent agents of Christ sacrificially giving their lives to bring salvation, education, and wholeness to unbelievers in a less-advanced culture. Wesley's mother had been deeply influenced by the biographies of Ziegenbalg and Plutschau, who served in south India with the Tranquebar Mission. This image of missions was an important aspect of John's early environment. The other model was that of church missionaries who saw themselves as international servants of the Church, much like the Roman Catholic missionaries today. Essentially it was this latter role that John Wesley was appointed to fill in Georgia. But he perceived missionary activity in an entirely different perspective: as the vehicle of his own spiritual growth. It was the medium in which his own devotion to Christ was nurtured and developed. Mission was not the end product of his discipleship, but the means to further it. Before his departure for Georgia, he wrote, "My chief motive (in going) is the hope of saving my own soul. I hope to learn the true sense of the gospel of Christ by preaching it to the heathen."[39] In words that would have charmed a Rousseau, he dreamed of a return to nature as the means for a return to grace.

In the Wesleyan instructional framework, the practical mission of the Church and the Word of God are bound into an interlocking nexus. The service involved in mission became the context, not only the result, of serious discipleship. For Wesley, the Bible was the practical equipment for the task at hand. Not only was it his message book, but also his method book. He held the Word of God in such awesome esteem that both the missionary and the recipient stood on equal footing before it. As a result there existed a profound solidarity between the messenger and the receiver of the Word.

A third development of Wesley's model was the provision for

upward mobility within a hierarchical system. The Anglican form of Church structure mirrored the class-conscious stratification of English society. Even the pew layout in the sanctuary was established according to an unchanging social order. However, the unsettled social situation in Georgia allowed Wesley an opportunity to operate on an egalitarian footing. While maintaining a ladder of leadership within his network of groups, he made it possible for adherents to move up the scale on the basis of faithfulness alone. The leaders of the basic groups by virtue of their leadership function became members of the next higher group regardless of their social rank, wealth, or education. Whatever Wesley's intentions in choosing this method, its later application in the Methodist Societies had drastic effects on the development of English social history. As will be demonstrated elsewhere, this provision for social advancement within the framework of the movement became a great leveling factor. The deterioration of the unofficial British caste system in the nineteenth century was furthered by the upward movement of Wesleyan group leaders in the eighteenth.[40]

One of the most valuable outcomes of the Georgia experiment was that Wesley's group technology underwent considerable improvement. He demonstrated that the pattern established in the Holy Club was transferable to other environments, with some modification. And, while in America, Wesley encountered two other forces which would significantly influence his instructional style: He renewed his acquaintance with an earlier group innovator, Mr. de Renty, and he was introduced to the Moravians.

THE DE RENTY MODEL

Although many diverse and disparate sources combined to form Wesley's group methodology, one of the earliest and most formative models for him was the small societies established in France by the Catholic nobleman Monr. de Renty. De Renty (1611-1649) had been strongly influenced by Thomas à Kempis's *Imitation of Christ*, and he kept a small copy with him at all times.[41] At age 27, de Renty had experienced a transforming awareness of the presence of Christ which led him to dedicate his whole life to caring for the poor and encouraging his countrymen to a devout and holy life.[42] These emphases certainly made de Renty an appealing model for Wesley, but what attracted him most was de Renty's method: small, intensely personal, and highly effective groups.

John Wesley became acquainted with de Renty's work through his father, Samuel, who admired the zeal, humility, and effectiveness of the Catholic saint. In a letter of encouragement to some Anglican Religious Societies in London in 1699, the elder Wesley cited de Renty's groups as evidence that group instruction was not a religious novelty.[43] Later, when young John was going to Georgia aboard the *Simmonds*, he read (perhaps re-read) de Renty's biography and found encouragement in the techniques he had utilized in his own ministry. In his journal for Friday, January 6, 1730, Wesley comments on both de Renty and his biographer:

> I ended the "Abridgment of Mr. de Renty's Life." O that such a life should be related by such an historian! who, by inserting all, if not more than all, the weak things that holy man ever said or did, by his commendation of almost every action or word which either deserved or needed it not, and by his injudicious manner of relating many others which were indeed highly commendable, has cast the shade of superstition and folly over one of the brightest patterns of heavenly wisdom.[44]

Throughout his life, Wesley continued to refer to de Renty as the epitome of Christian holiness coupled with concern for the poor and effective methodology. His frequent comments on the societies which de Renty had organized indicated that Wesley viewed them as a prototype of his own class meetings. Among the practices which Wesley selected from de Renty for emulation were:

1. A daily, detailed examination of that day's accomplishments and errors.[45]

2. The establishment of little gatherings of devout people who met weekly for prayer, reading devotional books, distribution of food to the poor, and discussion of personal religious experience.

3. The refusal to be treated as a person of high standing in society. (de Renty often did manual labor alongside the local workmen, a custom unheard of in high French society.)[46]

4. A zeal for personal holiness expressed in individual conduct and in practical service to others.

5. Carrying a cloth or sponge in his pocket to wash off offensive graffiti.[47]

6. The prescription of inexpensive remedies for those who could not afford doctors.[48]

In his "Further Appeal to Men of Reason and Religion," written to Roman Catholics, Wesley wrote: "O that you would follow that burning and shining light of your own Church, the Marquis de Renty!"[49] For the training of his own preachers, Wesley published his own extract of de Renty's biography, which he carefully abridged from 358 pages to 67.[50] This abridgment was a mainstay of Wesley's *Christian Library*, a set of fifty choice extracts.[51] Wesley frequently pointed his preachers to the section on de Renty's small groups, as follows:

> He earnestly desired to enlighten with the Knowledge of God, and inflame with his Love, the whole World; of which Paris being as it were an Epitome, he went thro' all the Quarters and Streets of that vast City, searching out what he could remove or bring in, for the Glory of God, and Salvation of Souls. And the same Spirit which moved him hereto, blest his Endeavors to rectify what

was amiss, and to strengthen what was right. This he did in so many several Ways, as a Man would think it impossible: But what cannot a Man do that is zealous, disinterested, and full of God?

2. He performed what possibly he could in his own Person, not sparing any Pains, nor losing one Moment: And where his Power fell short, he engaged others: And in all Places he labour'd, as much as in him lay, to induce such as desired to follow Christ, to join together, and assist one another in working out both their own and their Neighbour's Salvation. Many such Societies he establish'd at Caen, at Amiens, at Dijon, and in several parts of Burgundy; whose Endeavors being animated by a true Zeal for God, were bless'd with unexpected Success.[52]

Although there were similarities between the Religious Societies and de Renty's societies, there were also important distinctions.[53] The focus of the Anglican groups was personal growth through careful attention to themselves; de Renty concentrated on personal growth by ministering to the needs of others. The Anglicans hoped that Christian service would be the eventual outcome of their quest for personal holiness; de Renty viewed Christian service as the context in which personal holiness developed. Wesley gravitated towards the latter emphasis, keeping his groups well away from the mysticism and introspection of a self-centered group while maintaining the accountability of personal reporting on religious experience. Wesley recognized that preoccupation with one's personal spirituality could easily lead to that self-centeredness from which they were trying to escape. So, for Wesley, de Renty's model of growth-through-service enabled him to steer his groups around the dangers of morbid introspection and mysticism. Although Wesley could not have foreseen the perils which his fledgling Methodist groups would face, it was eventually the morass of subjectivity and mystical experience which would threaten the existence of his endeavors. And, thanks to de Renty, there was a sturdy component in his methodology which enabled Methodism to cope with its most severe challenge.

THE MORAVIANS

The Church of the Brethren (*Unitas Fratrum*) was a sect of German pietists who had been exiled from their ancestral home in the seventeenth century. During Wesley's time they lived in communal settlements on the estate of a wealthy nobleman in Saxony and had outposts in England and America. Because they were aliens and exiles, they were commonly known by nationality, rather than by their church affiliation, as "the Moravians."[54] They traced their spiritual ancestry back to Wyclif and Huss in Bohemia who were pre-Reformation evangelical preachers and reformers.

During the seventeenth century the pietists reacted to the cold and formal Lutheranism of Germany and sought to return to warm piety and devout simplicity of primitive Christianity, hence their name "Pietists."[55] Their emphasis was upon personal character and charitable works, and they showed little interest in or sympathy for systematic theology and classical learning. In their quest for personal fulfillment and Christian discipline, they had made several innovations in group instruction and interaction.

The first major leader of the Pietists was Philipp Jakob Spener, a Lutheran pastor at Frankfurt, who had been deeply influenced by the writings of Richard Baxter and other English Puritans.[56] Spener established home study groups for the pursuit of serious Christianity, which he called *collegia pietatis*. These groups later were gradually merged into the church itself and incorporated as functional units of Lutheran Pietism. Generally, they were discussion groups centered around the study of devotional books or the catechism.

Spener's successor was August Hermann Franke, a pastor who later became professor of theology at the new University of Halle. He combined Spener's emphasis on small groups with practical charity, forming orphan homes, charity schools, and a publishing company. The University of Halle blossomed into a teeming center of missionary activity and evangelistic outreach.[57]

Count Ludwig von Zinzendorf was a German nobleman who opened his estate to the exiled Moravians and became their spiritual leader. He had been reared under the influence of Spener and Franke and owed much to his Pietistic upbringing.[58] As a boy he had established little cell groups in his school for practical devotion, which he named "The Order of the Mustard Seed." This devotional club stressed Christian conduct as its unifying theme rather than any particular theology, and it later came to include a number of international notables, including General Oglethorpe, founder of the Georgia Colony in America. It was through this connection that General Oglethorpe offered land in America to the exiled Moravians.[59] The first group of twenty-six sailed for Georgia aboard the *Simmonds*, along with John and Charles Wesley.

John Wesley was immediately attracted to the Moravians, whom he dubbed "the Germans." Their simple lifestyle, sincere faith, and untiring service to the other passengers reminded him of the first-century Christians. However, it was especially the depth and majesty of their hymns that set Wesley to learning their language and spending time in conversation with the Moravians. He began to translate their hymns into English, and he included several of them in a book of hymns which he published at Charlestown in 1737.[60]

About ten days from its arrival in Georgia, the *Simmonds*, encountered a severe storm which nearly took the ship and its passengers to the bottom of the Atlantic. In the midst of the storm, Wesley developed a profound respect for these Moravian refugees. As he records in his journal,

> The sea broke over, split the mainsail in pieces, covered the ship, and poured in between decks, as if the great deep had already swallowed us up. A terrible screaming began among the English. The Germans calmly sang a hymn.[61]

This storm at sea was an unsettling experience for Wesley in several ways; it seems to have been the beginning of a turning point in his life.[62] The depth and tenacity of the Moravians' faith evoked Wesley's admiration, but it was also intimidating to him. He recognized that these unlettered and unknown Moravian exiles had a quality which was basic and essential to Christianity, but was totally beyond his grasp. He had studied theology and biblical literature in the original languages, given himself in charity and service, taken upon himself the reproach of his fellows for the sake of Christ, molded his life to a pattern of ascetic discipline, and yet had failed to find that simple faith which sustained the Moravians in the time of crisis. He had courage, but not faith, and he recognized that there was a world of difference between the two. His fascination with the Moravians drew him into long conversations with them concerning the secret of their inner confidence. He did not meet with them as the confident religious leader he had been in England; he was forced to admit their spiritual superiority and to accept the role of a humble learner.

The Moravians believed in another idea which was intimidating to Wesley: that individuals were granted salvation by God instantaneously, i.e., "born again," and could be assured of this divine favor by the subjective experience they called "the witness of the Spirit."[63] Their calm assurance of God's favor in contrast with the restlessness which Wesley was going through made him all the more miserable. Pastor Spangenburg, leader of the Georgia Moravians, asked Wesley directly if he was sure of his salvation, and Wesley fumbled for an appropriate answer. He recognized intellectually that this was in keeping with the experience of first-century Christians, but was embarrassed to admit that he had no such assurance. Isaac Taylor describes the perplexity of Wesley's relationship with the Moravians:

> At Oxford he had found himself stepping forward always in front of those around him. But on board the ship on which he crossed the Atlantic, and afterwards in the colony, he met with men who, without assuming a tone of arrogance toward him, spoke to him as a novice, and who, in the power of truth, brought his

conscience to a stand by questions which, while he admitted the pertinence of them, he could not answer with any satisfaction to himself. Thus it was that he returned to England in a state of spiritual discomfort and destitution. He had been stripped of that overweening religiousness upon which, as its basis, his ascetic egotism had hitherto rested. He rejoined his friends in a mood to ask and receive guidance, rather than to afford it.[64]

One practice which Wesley picked up from the Moravians almost led to his undoing, and certainly was a precipitating factor in his expulsion from the Georgia colony. The Moravians believed in determining God's will in difficult or unclear situations by casting lots. Wesley first applied this technique to a few minor decisions, then to the momentous choice whether or not to marry the daughter of one of the colonists, a Miss Sophey Hopkey. She was a very acceptable candidate for marriage to the young priest, and he was sufficiently fond of her to pursue marriage seriously. But the lot cast was against marriage. The normally unflappable Wesley was swept up in a confusion of reason, emotions, and the outcome of the lot. Miss Sophey promptly married someone else, and dear John handled the ensuing situation so ineptly that he was driven from the colony in near-disgrace.[65]

Defeated and disillusioned, he returned to England in January of 1738. He entered a period of restless discontent. He had bungled his opportunity for missionary service, his best prospect for marriage to date had slipped through his fingers because of his own clumsiness, but most of all he was suffering the loss of the conventional value system on which he had rested for security. He chafed under that sense of impotence that comes when the desired goal is within reach, but the means to attain it are not yet in sight. In his crisis of self-esteem, he turned again to the Moravians; this time to one of their pastors in London, Peter Bohler.

THE ALDERSGATE EXPERIENCE

It was the influence of the Moravians through the agency of Peter Bohler which led John Wesley to the heart of the Methodist phenomenon: the experience of personal conversion. Following his disheartening experience in Georgia, Wesley cast about London for several months in a quest for a source of spiritual security and meaning.[66] During this time he was counseled and encouraged by Bohler, the simple yet learned German pastor. They conversed in Latin concerning the nature of Christian faith, and Bohler urged Wesley to seek after an experience of instantaneous conversion as the solution to his personal dilemma. In characteristic fashion, the ever-logical Wesley first conducted a thorough examination of the accounts of conversions in the New Testament, concluding that a crisis moment of faith was the norm. Then he interviewed a number of people in London who claimed to have undergone such a transformation, and he decided that their professions were genuine. Their change of behavior, he concluded, could only be explained in terms of radical personal and spiritual transformation.[67] He now became convinced that this faith was a gift from God, and that God would surely bestow it upon every person who earnestly and perseveringly sought it. He resolved to seek it:

1. By absolutely renouncing all dependence, in whole or in part, upon my own works or righteousness; on which I had really grounded my hope of salvation, though I knew it not, from my youth up.

2. By adding to the constant use of all the other means of grace a continued prayer for this very thing: justifying, saving faith, a full reliance on the blood of Christ shed for me; a trust in Him, as my Christ, my sole justification, sanctification, and redemption.[68]

After weeks of relentless searching, Wesley finally found the experience he sought at a Moravian group meeting on Aldersgate Street in London. After the meeting, he wrote in his journal:

In the evening I went very unwilling to a society in Aldersgate Street, where one was reading Luther's *Preface to the Epistle to the Romans*. About a quarter before nine, while he was describing the change which God works in the heart through faith in Christ, I felt my heart strangely warmed. I felt I did trust in Christ, Christ alone, for salvation, and an assurance was given me, that He had taken away *my* sins, even *mine*, and saved *me* from the law of sin and death.[69]

This Wesleyan interpretation of conversion needs to be more narrowly defined than the normal psychological definition of "a change of direction following repentance." To the Methodists it was that and more. It is what God does in the life of a person who comes to him in penitent faith. It is that act by which a seeker becomes a finder, a religious servant becomes a spiritual son. This personal awareness of the assurance of God's favor was to become the cornerstone of the Methodist message and method.

Instantaneous conversion is not only a theological tenet and a matter of personal belief; it also has significant implications for religious instructional groups. It is the point of entry, the rite of passage, by which an individual becomes part of a distinct instructional process. Admittedly, historians have tended to look askance at religious conversions as verifiable historical data.[70] However, no competent analyst of eighteenth-century England would deny that those individuals who made up the Methodist movement entered it by claiming the same kind of transformation that Wesley underwent at Aldersgate. As Lecky, the noted English historian, pointed out,

It is scarcely an exaggeration to say that the scene which took place at that humble meeting in Aldersgate Street forms an epoch in English history; and that the conviction which then flashed upon one of the most powerful and most active intellects in England is the true source of English Methodism.[71]

Methodism was to be first of all, in Wesley's favorite terms, "heart-felt religion," not merely proper conduct, correct theology, or humanitarian service. From its beginnings in Wesley's conversion to its furthest outreach in ministry, the aims and methods of Methodism were constantly shaped by this experiential focus. Wesley himself valued the "born-again" experience so highly that he discounted all his earlier efforts as useless. Like Luther, he sharply distinguished religion built around moral conduct from religion based on faith. He explained this distinction in his journal:

> *June, 1740.* After we had wandered for many years in the new path of Salvation by faith and works, about two years ago it pleased God to show us the old way of Salvation by faith only.[72]

The happening at Aldersgate was so pivotal in Wesley's development that he began a new system of chronology in his journal starting from that date, May 24, 1738. From then on he frequently referred to events in terms of "*anno mea conversionis.*"[73]

The emphasis on instantaneous conversion was quickly and readily incorporated into Methodist hymnody. Charles Wesley, John's younger brother, composed a hymn, rich in autobiographical symbolism, to celebrate his brother's "new birth." Ever after, as Methodists gathered to sing their hymns, the theme of personal salvation by an act of faith was central.

As soon as Wesley had verified for his own life the necessity of conversion, he began preaching the same concept in churches and small groups wherever he could get an invitation. As he interpreted his own effectiveness in bringing about behavioral change in his hearers, he pointed to the teaching about instantaneous conversion as the motivational key:

> From the year 1725 to 1729 I preached much, but saw no fruit of my labour. Indeed, it could not be that I should; for I neither laid the foundation of repentance, nor of believing the gospel; taking it for granted, that all

to whom I preached were believers, and that many of them "needed no repentance." (2) From the year 1729 to 1734, laying a deeper foundation of repentance, I saw a little fruit. But it was only a little; and no wonder: for I did not preach faith in the blood of the Covenant. (3) From 1734 to 1738, speaking more of faith in Christ, I saw more fruit of my preaching and visiting from house to house, than ever I had done before; though I know not if any of those who were outwardly reformed were inwardly and thoroughly converted to God. (4) From 1738 to this time, speaking continually of Jesus Christ, laying Him only for the foundation of the whole building, making Him all in all, the first and the last; preaching only on this plan, "The kingdom of God is at hand; repent ye and believe the gospel;" the "word of God ran" as fire among the stubble; it "was glorified" more and more; multitudes crying out, "What must we do to be saved?" and afterwards witnessing, "By grace we are saved through faith."[74]

Julia Wedgwood, in her fine study of Wesley, states that "his regeneration transferred the birthday of a Christian from his baptism to his conversion, and in that change the partition line of the two great systems (Anglican and Methodist) is crossed."[75] Thus, conversion became the stock-in-trade of Methodism, its primary and fundamental method, upon which an elaborate instructional system would be built.

THE HERRNHUT MODEL

Swept up in his gratitude for Bohler's teaching on instantaneous conversion, Wesley decided immediately to trace the Moravian ideas to their European source. So, on July 4, 1738, (three weeks after his conversion) Wesley set out to visit the Moravian settlements in Saxony. At the first settlement, Marienborn, he met with the Moravian leader Count Zinzendorf. It appears from their later recollections that neither man was very impressed with the other,[76] but Wesley continued on in his search for clues to the Moravian uniqueness.

At the settlement of Herrnhut, Wesley observed the Moravian community with great fascination. Following a custom he had practiced since his student days at Oxford, he spent much of his time "collecting," or making terse observations and evaluations in a pocket notebook. His orderly mind revelled in their close administrative processes, and for three weeks he scrutinized their entire plan of operation, taking copious and meticulous notes. Count Zinzendorf had arranged the community into compact cells, or "bands" as he called them, for spiritual oversight and community administration.[77] The plan had been in operation for about eleven years at the time Wesley observed them. He noted in his journal:

II. The people of Herrnhut are divided:

1. Into five male classes, viz.: the little children, the middle children, the big children, the young men, and the married. The females are divided in the same manner.

2. Into eleven classes, according to the houses where they live. And in each class is an Helper, and Overseer, a Monitor, an Almoner, and a Servant.

3. Into about ninety bands, each of which meets twice a week at least, but most of them three times a week, to "confess their faults one to another, and pray for one another, that they may be healed...."[78]

9. The Church is so divided that first the husbands, then the widows, then the maids, then the young men, then the boys, then the girls, and lastly the little children, are in so many distinct classes; each of which is daily visited, the married men by a married man, the wives by a wife, and so of the rest. These larger are also (now) divided into near ninety smaller classes or bands, over each of

which one presides who is of the greatest experience. All these leaders meet the Senior every week, and lay open to him and to the Lord whatsoever hinders or furthers the work of God in the souls committed to their charge.[79]

Wesley especially appreciated the Moravian emphasis on personal character and charitable community involvement. They were simple, uncomplicated people, avoiding theological and classical learning in favor of personal and devotional growth. Their methodology was geared to promote collective interaction rather than individual achievement. This particularly appealed to Wesley, who viewed Christian conduct rather than some unified theology as the unifying theme of Christendom. In a letter to the Moravians at Herrnhut, Wesley commended their organizational plan and care of individuals: "I greatly approve of your conferences and bands; of your method of instructing children; and, in general, of your great care of the souls committed to your charge."[80]

One important element which the Moravians helped Wesley develop was an interest in the promotion of international missions. Wesley had first met the Moravians in Georgia in the context of overseas service, and he discovered at Herrnhut that this emphasis was woven into everything they did. The needs of world missions were kept continually before the people, and on special "Congregation Days" reports from overseas projects were cause for celebration.[81]

The Moravians practiced an educational distinction which was to become one of the hallmarks of Methodism: the separation of instruction from edification as two distinct functions. There were instructional sessions at Herrnhut called "choirs," and these were entirely given over to teaching. On the other hand, the bands were for personal encouragement, and no teaching was allowed during those meetings, only intimate sharing, confessions, and personal reporting of spiritual experience. Most religious education, both then and now, weave the two components together indiscriminately, but Wesley and the Moravians saw the advantage of keeping them apart and devising specific methodologies for each function.

Another contribution which Moravianism made to Methodism was the involvement of women in the service and ministry of the church. The gulf between clergy and laity was so vast in eighteenth-century Anglicanism that the exclusion of women from the clergy meant the virtual elimination of women from the leadership of the Christian community. As he analyzed the Herrnhut model which mobilized the entire Christian community for instruction and service, Wesley recognized the value of the inclusion of women in the instructional system. Nehemiah Curnock, editor of Wesley's journals, comments in a footnote to Wesley's Herrnhut observations:

> No doubt Wesley learned much at Herrnhut with reference to the employment of women in the church. We may trace to his friendship with the Moravians much of the early Methodist appreciation of women's gift for service amongst their sisters, and especially amongst the children.[82]

The Moravians also provided Wesley with the conceptual basis for organizational renewal within the Church of England. Count Zinzendorf had come to believe, as did Luther and Spener before him, that the way to restore and revitalize ecclesiastical organizations was the proliferation of independent renewal groups within the official framework of the larger organization. This was known among the pietists as "*ecclesiolae in ecclesia*,"[83] and in this approach Wesley recognized a means to bring new life to the stagnant structures of the Church of England. This approach to institutional renewal combined grassroots initiative with episcopal leadership to maintain a vigorous balance between spontaneity and order, enthusiasm and established authority.

Wesley returned to England with zeal for his new-found techniques, eager to try them out on religious seekers in the London area. Within a few weeks of his return, he had organized bands of believers after the Moravian/Herrnhut model. He wrote back to his friends and mentors at Herrnhut, reporting his success:

> Glory be to God, even the Father of our Lord Jesus Christ, for His unspeakable gift for giving me to be an eye-witness of your faith, and love, and holy conversation in Christ Jesus! I have borne testimony thereof with all plainness of speech in many parts of Germany, and thanks have been given to God by many on your behalf.
>
> We are endeavoring here also, by the grace which is given us, to be followers of you, as ye are of Christ. Fourteen were added to us since our return, so that we have now eight bands of men, consisting of fifty-six persons; all of whom seek for salvation only in the blood of Christ. As yet we have only two small bands of women; the one of three and the other of five persons. But there are many others who only wait till we have leisure to instruct them how they may most effectually build up one another in the faith and love of Him who gave Himself for them.[84]

Despite his enthusiasm for the methodological and organizational innovations he had borrowed from the Moravians, Wesley had begun to have some serious doubts of their doctrines and practices. Several members of the Oxford "Holy Club" had joined the Moravians, and one of them, John Gambold, became their first English bishop. However, Wesley's reservations soon led to tensions with the Moravian Brethren, and ultimately a final separation. By 1741, the break was nearly complete, as he wrote to his brother Charles:

> As yet I dare in no wise join with the Moravians: (1) Because their general scheme is mystical, not scriptural; refined in every point above what is written, immeasurably beyond the plain gospel. (2) Because there is darkness and closeness in all their behaviour, and guile in

almost all their words. (3) Because they not only do not practice, but utterly despise and decry, self-denial and the daily cross. (4) Because they conform to the world, in wearing gold and gay or costly apparel. (5) Because they are by no means zealous of good works, or at least only to their own people. For these reasons (chiefly) I will rather, God being my helper, stand quite alone than join with them; I mean till I have full assurance that they are better acquainted with "the truth as it is in Jesus."[85]

Wesley's acknowledged debt of gratitude to the Moravians made this controversy with them a painful one,[86] but he stood by his doctrinal principles and broke completely with his spiritual and methodological mentors. Nevertheless, he had gained invaluable insights from them that would be incorporated into his overall instructional system. The chart on page 64 illustrates those Moravian practices and beliefs Wesley liked and adapted as well as those he disliked and avoided.

THE FETTER LANE SOCIETY

One of the most significant group experiments undertaken by Wesley leading up to the Methodist system in its final form was the Fetter Lane Society. This gathering of forty or fifty people, mostly Germans, met for prayer and group encouragement on Wednesday nights in London, beginning on May 1, 1738.[87] It was formed as an updated Religious Society associated with the Church of England, but it was substantially altered in form and method by innovations borrowed from the Moravians. Wesley shared the leadership of the group with Moravian Peter Bohler. In order to maintain the original vision of this group, a list of thirty-three articles was drawn up, consisting mostly of rules for group admission, function, cohesion, expulsion, and order. (See Appendix B.) It is fascinating that although no guidelines were given for the content of these meetings, great care was exercised in their organizational pattern. For example, the rules dictated minute details of procedure, such as:

THE MORAVIAN LEGACY
TO WESLEY'S METHODOLOGY

Elements Wesley liked	Elements Wesley disliked
• Hymn-singing as a form of instruction	• Lack of openness, frankness, and simplicity in speech
• Women's place of service	• Exclusiveness
• Special services: "Agape Feast," Watchnights, etc.	• Domination by Zinzendorf
• "ecclesiolae in ecclesia"	• Antinomianism
• Intense fellowship: unity before information	• The Moravian doctrine of "stillness"
• Emphasis on conduct, no speculation	• Downgrading the "means of grace," like communion and baptism
• Emphasis on instantaneous conversion, assurance of salvation	• Making decisions by casting lots
• Simplicity of lifestyle	• A tendency toward mysticism
• Distinction of choirs for instruction and bands for edification	• Subjective piety unrelated to human affairs

14. That exactly at ten, if the Business of the Night be not finished, a short concluding Prayer be used, that those may go who are in haste, but that all depart the Room by half an Hour after ten.

15. That whosoever speaks in this Conference stand up, and that none else speak till he is set down.

16. That nothing which is mentioned in this Conference be by any Means mentioned out of it.[88]

As the new society began to take shape, it was noticeably different from Wesley's earlier models in several respects. First of all, in this new society there was no rule which confined membership to those who belonged to the Church of England.[89] This was, in its day, a radical departure from established custom, especially for a staunch churchman like Wesley. In fact, it was actually against the law in England for such interdenominational religious groups to meet at all, and this illegality would become a threat to the group's existence, almost before it got underway. A corollary to this open membership rule was the absence of any requirement of regular attendance at the services and rituals of the Church of England, a feature which was conspicuous in the earlier Religious Societies.

At this point in Wesley's life he was dissatisfied with all the existing group forms he had tried, but in this new society he was able to combine effective elements from several methodologies to forge a powerful synthesis. The formation of the Fetter Lane Society also signaled the attainment of a new plateau in his comprehension of group dynamics. His own spiritual pilgrimage had compelled him to seek and/or establish an atmosphere conducive to the cultivation of the inner life. Although he had been a frequent participant in the Religious Societies, they frustrated him by their lack of opportunity to bare one's soul, to share one's spiritual struggles in a secure and accepting group. Although these Religious Society meetings had stimulated his thinking and whetted his spiritual appetite, he had had to limit his intimate discussions to informal conversations outside the structure of the groups. In the format of the Fetter Lane Society, he sought to bring the process of personal struggle under the formal umbrella of group order and provide a protective environment where that struggle could produce maximum growth. The resultant group structure was not quite the impressive system which would be fully developed later in the Methodist Societies, but it seems to have been by far the most ingenious plan for personal religious development yet devised in England.

The Fetter Lane Society brought together the strengths of both the Anglican Religious Societies and the Moravian bands. The Religious Societies were particularly well-designed for effective cognitive instruction, especially the acquisition of religious information for personal application. The Moravian bands established an optimum environment for the development of personal devotion and the cultivation of a radical lifestyle. Rather than combine these two approaches into one omnibus group methodology, sacrificing the uniqueness of each, Wesley yoked them together as tandem elements within a controlled system.[90] The entire society was to meet at 8:00 on Wednesday evenings in a large room for instruction and inspiration. The leader was Bohler or Wesley or perhaps a visiting speaker, and they stuck closely to the lecture format. Group discussion was not encouraged. The only response the participants made may have been affirmative nods and occasional amens.

In order to keep the instructional function entirely separate from the "internalization" function, separate bands of five to ten people of the same sex were assigned to meet twice weekly in addition to the Wednesday session of the society.[91] Their purpose was to provide an environment in which intimate interaction could be fostered. By controlling the elements of the group process through a set of published norms, Wesley was able to facilitate a certain set of outcomes in terms of personal spiritual growth. In these bands, lay leaders appointed by Wesley and Bohler directed the flow of conversation by a set of predetermined questions. As each member spoke in turn and reported the state of his or her religious life, the rest of the group was to respond appropriately in terms of encouragement, affirmation, suggestions, and support. By these questions total participation was attained in two ways: (1) each person stated his or her own condition at every meeting, and (2) every listener was expected to give verbal or nonverbal response to all other members as they spoke. By tailoring the methodology to fit the instructional mode, and by keeping the group functions separate, Wesley was able to combine the strengths of both modes, society and band.

The use of unordained and untrained laymen as band leaders was a shocking innovation to Anglican culture, and soon provoked waves of criticism from both the established clergy and the general public. No doubt the Moravian influence was instrumental in bringing about this leadership innovation, since they strongly believed in the universal priesthood of believers.[92] In their native Germany in the more orthodox Lutheran churches, the pastor played a role of complete pre-eminence, to the virtual exclusion of lay people from all ministerial functions. In Wesley's day, this was also generally true of the Anglican clergy. They were a professional elite. In reaction to the elitism of their Lutheran colleagues, the Moravians spread the ministerial responsibility for worship, instruction, and service very broadly across the entire congregation. All members were expected to carry their part of the priestly role, and the entire community was mobilized in a ministerial corps. In somewhat the same manner, band leaders in the Fetter Lane Society received valuable experience in group leadership. And participants in the bands were more open to speak their true feelings once they perceived that their group leaders were peers, not superiors. Whatever the cost in terms of public outcry, this investment in lay leadership turned out to be a wise and productive innovation for Wesley.

This new Society at Fetter Lane was more careful in the admission of new members than were other voluntary societies Wesley had known. The thirty-three articles of group conduct were read aloud to new applicants, who had to make a public commitment to the rules before they were admitted on probation.[93] The probation period lasted two months. Other members in the society had the right to voice opposition to any new applicant, and new members could be excluded by the consensus of the membership. No longer was the focus of authority in the professional leader; the group itself now had the power to include or exclude its own members.

As Wesley and Bohler drew up the rules governing the Fetter Lane Society, a new rationale was presented to justify the existence of such a group project. For the first time an appeal was made to Scripture as the basis for an interactive fellowship. The preamble states that this initiative was begun "In Obedience to the Command of God by St. James."[94] Never before had Wesley suggested that the origin of such groups was to be found in Scripture, but from this point onward he would argue that his particular group structure was not only allowed, but also prescribed by the Bible. And, as the groups developed, Wesley saw in them more and more the pattern of fellowship which characterized the primitive church.

For the next two years, John Wesley's base of ministry was in the Fetter Lane Society. It was an unwieldy admixture of various religious persuasions—Anglican, Moravian, and those who had been influenced by French mystics—but Wesley's firm administrative hand managed to keep tension from destroying the group. He dealt privately and individually with those whose behavior threatened to disrupt the cohesion of the fellowship. However, as his renown as a preacher spread, his speaking engagements led him farther and farther afield. Often he would be absent from the Society for weeks at a time. During these absences, regardless of who was left in charge, the substitutes could not ameliorate the warring factions as Wesley could.[95] Finally, a point was reached in July of 1740 when even Wesley himself could not prevent dissolution. Even though Wesley was grieved over the termination of his relationship with the Fetter Lane Society, his two years' experience had been invaluable in the development of his own group strategy, and further innovation would probably have been difficult to bring about without leaving the society.

The Fetter Lane Society represented a significant plateau in the development of Wesley's group methodology. The two levels of participation, the band and the society, allowed for two separate educational strategies each with its own structure and content. The following chart displays the contrasting functions of the two instructional modes within the Fetter Lane Society:

A Summary of Instructional Elements In The
Fetter Lane Society

	BAND	SOCIETY
PURPOSE:	overt behavioral change	cognitive acquisition
LEADERS:	lay leadership	professional leadership
LEADERSHIP FUNCTION:	leader as enabler	leader as instructor
METHODS AND TECHNIQUES:	personal interaction 5-10 members one sex active participation confession of struggle every person spoke subjective emphasis appointed membership	lecture/sermon 50-100 members both sexes passive response biblical presentation only the leader spoke objective emphasis membership by choice
PHILOSOPHICAL/ THEOLOGICAL ASSUMPTIONS:	Moravian precedents priesthood of all God as immanent faith as experiential	Anglican precedents priesthood of elite God as transcendent faith as inferential

The two-tiered structure of the Fetter Lane Society model provided a pattern for group interaction that Wesley would employ in his public ministry among the unchurched masses. At this point, he did not have complete control over this particular society, so he was not free to experiment with variations. However, some radical changes were about to take place in his life which would give him the opportunity to develop his own instructional system and to control it completely.

FIELD PREACHING

As discussed at length in chapter 1, the technique of "field preaching"—outdoor religious rallies—opened a vast untapped audience to the Wesleyan message. From the vantage point of the twentieth century, such a method seems hardly novel or unconventional, but it stood in marked contrast to accepted religious practice in Wesley's day.

Also notable are contrasts between the personal styles of Whitefield and the Wesleys. Whitefield was of an entirely different temperament than either of the Wesleys. His Georgia experience was much more pleasant and profitable than theirs. George's mother had been an innkeeper,[96] and as a youth he had learned those skills of tact and graciousness indispensable to public service. The Wesleys, on the other hand, had known nothing but the sheltered parsonage and the academic community at Oxford prior to their missionary service. They eventually learned the tact essential for interpersonal cooperation, but it came much later and at the cost of a great deal of grief. Whitefield's strong preaching was augmented by a very practical turn of mind and excellent personal diplomacy. Even amongst the soldiers aboard ship, he charmed his way into their confidence and had the roughest of them singing hymns, offering prayers, and repeating the catechism by the time they reached Georgia.[97] The very settlers which Wesley had alienated by his offensive high-churchmanship, Whitefield brought into regular worship and some degree of piety. For example, Whitefield baptized by sprinkling some children whose parents had forbidden Wesley to baptize, because he insisted on immersion even in the dead of winter.[98]

Despite all that John Wesley needed to learn to minister to the masses at Bristol and elsewhere, he evidently succeeded. As noted in chapter 1, this success afforded him opportunity to further test his ideas about small-group discipleship. He reformed the Religious Societies in Bristol, dividing them into bands as in the Fetter Lane Society. At Society meetings he "expounded" or instructed the people on various elements of an ethical Christian lifestyle, especially calling their attention to the ethical standard of the Sermon on the Mount and the pattern of the early church as recorded in the Book of Acts. In the bands, all members gave account weekly of the progress of their spiritual and personal development.

These questions may be asked, "What difference does it make whether Wesley did his preaching in a church or in a coal pit? What influence does that bear on his instructional methodology?" The difference is in the target population, and in this case it was a vital difference in strategy. Wesley wanted above everything else to find a remedy to the moral ills of his time and nation. This was reflected in the goal-slogan he adopted as his watchword: "To spread scriptural holiness throughout the land." Wesley took his appeal to the common people of England, and on their own turf and in their own terminology. In the preface to one of his volumes of sermons, he indicates how completely he jettisoned the gentleman's world of Oxford in order to adapt his thinking to his working-class audience:

3. I design plain truth for plain people; therefore, of set purpose, I abstain from all nice and philosophical speculations; from all perplexed and intricate reasonings; and, as far as possible, from even the show of learning, unless in sometimes citing the original Scripture. I labour to avoid all works which are not easy to be understood, all which are not used in common life; and, in particular, those kinds of technical terms that so frequently occur in Bodies of Divinity; those modes of speaking which men of reading are acquainted with, but which to common people are an unknown tongue....

4. Nay, my design is, in some sense, to forget all that ever I have read in my life. I mean to speak, in the general, as if I had never read one author, ancient or modern (always excepting the one inspired). I am persuaded, that, on the one hand, this may be a means of enabling me more clearly to express sentiments of my heart, while I simply follow the chain of my own thoughts,

without entangling myself with those of other men; and that, on the other, I shall come with fewer weights upon my mind, with less of prejudice and prepossession, either to search for myself, or to deliver to others, the naked truths of the Gospel.[99]

Thus, Wesley's choice of the common working people as his target audience dictated some of the criteria by which his instructional tools would be shaped. His language would be concrete rather than abstract, his appeal would be almost entirely based on Scripture rather than Scripture plus the accumulated thoughts of the learned, and his group techniques would be geared to elicit behavioral response rather than intellectual dialogue. Taking his message to the open fields necessitated an entirely different instructional method than had worked at Oxford or even among the Moravian/Anglican groups which met in London.

THE FOUNDERY SOCIETY

Wesley's instructional system reached its final stage of development with the establishment of the Foundery Society in December of 1739. During a three-year organizational period, several new features were added to the Wesleyan format of group instruction, but once that pattern was established, it remained largely unchanged during the remaining fifty years of Wesley's ministry. The subsequent history of Methodism in the eighteenth century relates primarily to the replication of this pattern in various locations, both in England and abroad. In terms of Wesley's "instructional biography," the period from his birth in 1703 to 1743 may be called the *developmental* stage of his system; 1743-1793 is the *implementation* stage.

In the fall of 1739, Wesley was still a member and a leader of the Fetter Lane Society in London, but he was experiencing great difficulties in holding the dissenting factions together. The mystical Moravian element, the party influenced by the French prophets, and the traditional Anglicans were pulling in opposite directions. Wesley divided his time between the feuding society and preaching in the open public gathering places in London, an activity he greatly preferred. Late in the year, as he was preaching in an open meadow called Moorfields, he was approached by two businessmen with the offer of a nearby facility.

> 90. In November, 1739, two gentlemen, then unknown to me, (Mr. Ball and Mr. Watkins), came and desired me, once and again, to preach in a place called the Foundery, near Moorfields. With much reluctance I at length complied. I was soon after pressed to take that place into my own hands. Those who were most earnest therein lent me the purchase-money, which was one hundred and fifteen pounds....

> 91. The united society began a little after....[100]

The Foundery had been the armory where the royal cannon were cast, but an explosion in 1716 had destroyed the building, and it lay in a heap of ruins until Wesley bought and rebuilt it.[101] By June 1740, the building was finished enough to accommodate a sizable audience as well as to provide housing for the evangelists. Wesley saw in the starting of this new facility the opportunity to make some needed changes in his methodology.

For several months Wesley had chafed under a sense of dissatisfaction with the group methods he had been using. When he visited Oxford in October he was distressed to discover that the efforts of the now-defunct Holy Club and the withering Religious Societies had failed to produce a lasting change in the community.

> I had a little leisure to take a view of the shattered condition of things here. The poor prisoners, both in the castle and in the city prisons, had now none that cared for their souls; none to instruct, advise, comfort, and build them up in the knowledge and love of the Lord Jesus. None was left to visit the warehouses, where also we used to meet with the most moving objects of com-

passion. Our little school, where about twenty poor children at a time had been taught for many years, was on the point of being broken up, there being none now either to support or to attend it; and most of those in the town, who were once knit together, and strengthened one another's hands in God, were torn asunder and scattered abroad. *"It is time for Thee, Lord, to lay to Thy hand."*[102]

Even the Fetter Lane Society, improvement as it was on the former models, had major structural deficiencies. First of all, its leadership pattern was too unstable; the "director" was elected by vote of the membership and could be removed by vote at any time. This weakness allowed doctrinal issues to swamp the society's proceedings and enable impulsive and reactionary members to dominate the meetings. Another weakness, by Wesley's assessment, was that the Fetter Lane Society reached only a very limited population of highly-motivated church people. In his experience with field preaching, Wesley recognized the need for a tool or method by which to assimilate the newly-evangelized masses into the mainstream of the church. Another related frustration had to do with the moral ills of society; the Religious Societies had been bold to speak out against injustice and immorality, but they had no effective means of addressing those problems directly. They could make pronouncements about the needs, but they could not reach the people with the means of rehabilitation or reconstruction. Wesley recognized that this was essentially a management problem, a case of faulty design. The Fetter Lane Society was too far gone to be rescued by remedial measures, but Wesley saw an opportunity to start from "the ground floor" in a new location. The new model enabled Methodism to shape the destiny of England's working class.

In the preface to the *Rules* of this new society, Wesley describes its origin and rationale:

1. In the latter end of the year 1739, eight or ten persons came to me in London, who appeared to be deeply con-

vinced of sin, and earnestly groaning for redemption. They desired (as did two or three more the next day) that I would spend some time with them in prayer, and advise them how to flee from the wrath to come; which they saw continually hanging over their heads; That we might have more time for this great work, I appointed a day when they might all come together; which from thenceforward, they did every week, namely, on Thursday, in the evening. To these, and as many more as desired to join with them (for their number increased daily) I gave those advices, from time to time, which I judged most needful for them; and we always concluded our meeting with prayer suited to their several necessities.

2. This was the rise of the United Society, first at London and then in other places. Such a Society is no other than "a company of men having the form, and seeking the power, of godliness; united, in order to pray together, to receive the word of exhortation, and to watch over one another in love, that they may help each other to work out their salvation."[103]

Wesley continued to preach outdoors almost daily to large crowds that gathered in the open plain at Moorfields, and as people showed evidence of sincere interest, Wesley invited them to meetings at the nearby Foundery, still under construction. Early in the year (1740) a new feature was added to the program of the Foundery Society: early morning Bible expositions. In his missionary experiment in Georgia, Wesley had attempted this kind of service, since he felt it was reminiscent of the practice of the primitive church. Seeing the advantage of such a service, he began to expound on passages of Scripture in a short meeting, beginning at 5:00 a.m., before the workers were due at their jobs. By June, when the building was ready, over 300 members were meeting regularly as "The United Society," Wesley's name for the new venture. Shortly after, he made a complete and final break with the Fetter Lane Society, and eighteen or nineteen of its members joined him at the Foundery. As he had done in earlier experiments, Wesley gathered the most serious seekers into bands for personal and intimate sharing of their religious experiences.

The new building was a new beginning for Wesley. He now had his own building and a society of his own making; it was neither Moravian nor Anglican, but a distinctly new hybrid. It contained elements of all that he had experienced before, but it was different than and superior to all the previous models. In addition to the establishment of a society for instruction and bands for edification, Wesley made some other important modifications. In order to open the membership to a wider target population, the only requirement for admission to the new society was "a desire to flee from the wrath to come, to be saved from their sins." The old exclusion clauses which had barred outsiders from the Religious Societies were replaced by an open admission policy. The early morning Bible lessons were a new feature, as was the close linkage between the society and field preaching.

One part of the Foundery experiment that was tried and failed was Wesley's house-to-house visitation program, a technique he had borrowed from his father, Samuel Wesley.

> My father's method was to visit all his parishioners, sick or well, from house to house, to talk with each of them on the things of God and observe severally the state of their souls. What he then observed he minuted down in a book kept for that purpose. In this manner he went through his parish (which was near three miles long) three times. He was visiting it the fourth time round when he fell into his last sickness.[104]

His father had called his practice *Notitia Parochialis*.[105] The personal contact was very helpful to the younger Wesley, but it took too much time; he could not continue his other duties and regularly visit all those who needed help. He was always ready to try new methods and equally quick to abandon them if they did not work.

Wesley recognized the need for a way to give personal oversight to the growing numbers of members, and his frustration only heightened his readiness for a truly workable method.

> II. 1. But as much as we endeavored to watch over each other, we soon found some who did not live in the gospel. I do not know that any hypocrites were crept in; for indeed there was no temptation: But several grew cold, and gave way to the sins which had long easily beset them. We quickly perceived there were many ill consequences of suffering these to remain among us. It was dangerous to others; inasmuch as all sin is of an infectious nature. It brought such a scandal on their brethren as exposed them to what was not properly the reproach of Christ. It laid a stumbling-block in the way of others, and caused the truth to be evil spoken of.
>
> 2. We groaned under these inconveniences long, before a remedy could be found. The people were scattered so wide in all parts of the town, from Wapping to Westminster, that I could not easily see what the behavior of each person in his own neighbourhood was: So that several disorderly walkers did much hurt before I was apprized of it.[106]

Charles Wesley had been ministering to societies in Bristol and Kingswood, and at John's encouragement he began to cut the ties linking those societies with the Moravian and Anglican Societies. Charles added his own innovation to the "United Societies" format after exclusion from Anglican churches in Bristol: He began administering the Lord's Supper in society gatherings. With these new societies under his control, John Wesley demonstrated his managerial ability by delegating as much responsibility to Society participants as he could. Those who could handle finances were appointed "stewards," those with special graces of compassion he named "sick-visitors," and those who could expound the Scriptures were appointed as "lay assistants."

One of the most helpful changes was a new way to enable local leaders to have a voice in the control of Society membership. Wesley compiled lists of people who wanted to join the Society and he presented these lists to the combined bands for their approval. As he read each name, any band member could raise an objection or voice particular approval. If there was sound reason why any person should not be admitted, that person was brought face-to-face with his or her accusers. If prospective members repented, or if the accusations were unfounded, they were admitted on two months' trial. If they were belligerent, or refused to work on their problem, they were not admitted. Admission was controlled by the issuing of tickets, signed by Wesley himself.

> 2. To each of those of whose seriousness and good con-versation I found no reason to doubt I gave a testimony under my own hand by writing their name on a ticket prepared for that purpose, every ticket implying as strong recommendation of the person to whom it was given as if I had wrote at length, "I believe the bearer hereof to be one that fears God and works righteousness."

> 3. Those who bore these tickets _____ (these or tessarae, as the ancients termed them, being of just the same force with the _____ _____, "commendatory letters," mentioned by the Apostle), wherever they came, were acknowledged by their brethren and received with all cheerfulness. These were likewise of use in other respects. By these it was easily distinguished, when the Society were to meet apart, who were members of it and who not. These also supplied us with a quiet and inoffensive method of removing any disorderly member. He has no new ticket at the quar-terly visitation (for so often the tickets are changed),

and hereby it is immediately known that he is no longer of the community.[107]

The tickets were good for three months; after which all members of the society were interviewed to determine their fitness for continuing as members in good standing. By this measure, the quality of participation was insured. It is interesting to note that the focus is not on agreement with the leaders' doctrine or even on moral perfection, but on the willingness to cooperate with the group guidelines for participation. Members of the Society could be in disagreement with the leadership and also be struggling with serious moral problems and still be welcome participants. But, they could not remain in the Society if their behavior threatened the cohesion of the group or blocked its normal function.

By June of 1741 the Foundery Society had grown to 900 members, the Bristol/Kingswood work was growing steadily, and new societies were being established in the Mid-lands and as far north as Newcastle-on-Tyne. The bands were not increasing in number as rapidly as the societies, and Wesley was concerned about the need for better supervision. The method which sprang up to fill this void was created by a sea-captain in the Bristol Society during a financial drive. Wesley described the origin of the well-known class meeting methodology:

> 3. At length, while we were thinking of quite another thing, we struck upon a method for which we have cause to bless God ever since. I was talking with several of the Society in Bristol concerning the means of paying the debts there, when one stood up and said, "Let every member of the Society give a penny a week till all are paid." Another answered, "But many of them are poor, and cannot afford to do it." "Then," said he, "put eleven of the poorest with me; and if they can give anything, well: I will call on them weekly; and if they can give nothing, I will give for them as well as for myself. And each of you call on eleven of your neighbours weekly;

receive what they give, and make up what is wanting." It was done. In a while, some of these informed me, they found such and such an one did not live as he ought. *It struck me immediately, "This is the thing; the very thing we have wanted so long."* I called together all the Leaders of the classes (so we used to term them and their companies), and desired that each would make a particular inquiry into the behaviour of those whom he saw weekly. They did so. Many disorderly walkers were detected. Some turned from the evil of their ways. Some were put away from us. Many saw it with fear, and rejoiced unto God with reverence.

5. It is the business of a Leader (1) To see each person in his class, once a week at the least, in order to inquire how their souls prosper; to advise, reprove, comfort, or exhort, as occasion may require; to receive what they are willing to give toward the relief of the poor. (2) To meet with the Minister and the Stewards of the Society, in order to inform the Minister of any that are sick, or of any that are disorderly and will not be reproved; to pay to the Stewards what they have received of their several classes in the week preceding.[108]

The class meeting filled the critical gap between the society and the bands. It was soon the most prominent and unique feature of early Methodism and was copied by other religious groups as well as by political, commercial, and educational organizations.[109] To this cluster of group modes, Wesley added two more during this formative period: (1) The first was a "select society," originally for the most ardent seekers after personal holiness. The function of strategic planning later became an additional feature of this group. (2) A final group called the "penitent band" was a rehabilitation program, much like today's Alcoholics Anonymous, which dealt with people who had severe social and moral problems and required more stringent and forceful treatment.

The Foundery Society was soon looked upon as the mother-church of Methodism. Wherever people responded to the Wesleyan message, they were gathered into an organization following the Foundery Society pattern. Wesley's methodology continued to undergo minor alterations, but the pattern remained basically unchanged throughout his lifetime. The details of each of the interlocking groups, the duties of leaders, and the characteristics peculiar to each part of the system will be discussed in the following chapter.

CHAPTER THREE

Wesley's System of Interlocking Groups

The instructional components of the Methodist system were fully assembled by 1742. Over the next fifty years, during the period of Methodist expansion under Wesley's personal leadership, the structure of the groups underwent only slight alterations. Wesley's physical presence in the societies, made possible by his constantly revolving itinerancy, kept the structure of the system close to his original vision. Alongside the instructional system was an administrative system which increased in complexity as the Methodist movement grew and expanded. The two systems overlapped at points, but, at least during Wesley's lifetime, the instructional pattern was quite stable.

Much of the effectiveness of this hierarchy of instructional groups was due to the fact that each component gathering of people employed methods tailored to a specific function; then those groups were yoked together into an interlocking network. Probably the best way to distinguish between each group in the chain is to refer to each category as a specific educational mode, if we understand the term "mode" to mean "an appropriate method of procedure."

THE SOCIETY: THE COGNITIVE MODE

The Methodist society was the group which included all the Methodists in a given area or locality. The term "society" is nearly synonymous with the term "congregation." It included all those who were official members plus any adherents who attended open functions of the fellowship. The Methodist society was the focal point of group identification. In relation to the other groups within the Methodist system, the society was the hub of all other functions; it was the "umbrella" group of the organization in that all other related groups came under its jurisdiction. In the *Rules of the United Societies*, Wesley gives his own definition of a society:

> Such a society is no other than a company of men having the form and seeking the power of godliness, united in order to pray together, to receive the word of exhortation, and to watch over one another in love, that they may help each other to work out their own salvation.[1]

The primary function of the society was cognitive instruction; it was the educational channel by which the tenets of Methodism were presented to the target population. Those who had been drawn to the Methodists by curiosity or by field preaching or by the invitation of a friend were introduced to its particular teachings through society meetings. The methods selected for this mode were as appropriate for large-group presentation as could be obtained in that day and time: lecture, preaching, public reading, hymn singing, and "exhorting." In each case the physical arrangement was an audience of fifty or more people, arranged in rows, usually listening to a speaker give a prepared talk. Little or no provision was made in this particular mode for personal response or feedback.

The learning environment for this cognitive process was the Methodist chapel, a plain, austere building with no musical instruments and with separate seating for men and women.[2] Although many of the earliest Methodist societies met in rented halls, the pattern of building their own chapels was soon the rule rather than the exception. In contrast to the Anglican churches and cathedrals, where even the arrangement of pews reflected the stratified social order, the Methodist chapels were filled on a first-come-first-served basis, eliminating any social distinctions. When fine ladies and cultured gentlemen attended Methodist meetings, which they often did, they had no advantage in seating over the rough miners, soldiers, or factory workers with whom they shared a backless bench.

The meetings of the Wesleyan societies were carefully scheduled so as not to conflict with any of the services of the Church of England. This widely-acclaimed feature was a calculated symbol of Methodism's submissive and subordinate role to the Church and its supplementary nature. The tacit message conveyed by the schedule was, "We are loyal Anglicans and not in competition or opposition to the Church of England."

Since the central unit of the Methodist system served essentially cognitive ends, it was inevitable that a body of concepts would soon come to be recognized as "Methodist doctrine." Wesley was primarily concerned with methodology; his definition of a Methodist was "one who lives according to the *method* laid down in the Bible."[3] However, even though he may not have set out to become a theological innovator,[4] what remains today of Methodism is an organization and that body of doctrine which came to be associated with the early Methodist societies. As Marshall McLuhan has theorized, "The medium is the message."[5] In this case, the medium is the whole arrangement of Methodist groups; the message is the selection of ideas, all current in England at the time, which were germane to that medium.

There is a voluminous literature on the distinctive concepts related to Wesleyanism, and there is no need to examine those analyses in depth. There are, however, a few key concepts which Wesley held, and which were related to his methods to such an extent that they should at least be mentioned. In several points, Wesley refused to accept popular beliefs, especially concerning the nature of humanity and society, and hammered out his own set of foundational principles. The relevance to his instructional methodology is that his belief system formed a selection grid or filter by which he either selected, rejected, or modified educational tools as he became aware of them. Some of his key themes are:

1. *The perfectibility of humanity.* In contrast to pessimism about human nature which was characteristic of

the Reformed or Calvinistic churchmen, Wesley was optimistic that human nature could be radically altered for the better. In this sense, he was like Professor Huxley who held that "perfectibility is the one rational goal of progressive existence."[6] This is not to be confused with the humanism of the Enlightenment—concepts which advocated that human beings could raise themselves by their own efforts (Wesley had dabbled in that during his days at Oxford and rejected it), but rather the perfection of humanity's intentions and behavior by God's grace.

2. *The freedom of the human will.* Against the prevalent tide of theological determinism found in both Anglican and Dissenting churches, Wesley rejected the fatalistic idea that all human actions are predetermined. He placed the responsibility for human behavior squarely on the individual, whom he believed to be capable of making moral choices. The proper name for this belief is Arminianism, a system of thought with which Wesley identified fairly completely.[7]

3. *True religion manifests itself in human relationships.* In contrast to the mystics, who emphasized inner contemplation as the way to spiritual growth, Wesley promoted social interaction as the way to "holiness." His *Preface to the 1739 Hymnbook* is a classic refutation of mysticism and solitary religion, placing the full thrust of personal growth on group participation.

> Directly opposite to this [mysticism] is the Gospel of Christ. Solitary religion is not to be found there. "Holy solitaries" is a phrase no more consistent with the Gospel than holy adulterers. The Gospel of Christ knows of no religion, but social; no holiness, but social holiness. Faith working by love is the

length and breadth and depth and height of
Christian perfection. This commandment
have we from Christ, that he who loves God,
love his brother also; and that we manifest
our love by doing good unto all men, especially to them that are of the household of
faith. And, in truth, whosoever loveth his
brethren not in word only, but as Christ
loved him, cannot but be zealous of good
works. He feels in his soul a burning, restless
desire of spending and being spent for them.
My Father, will he say, worketh hitherto, and
I work: and, at all possible opportunities, he
is, like his Master, going about doing good.[8]

When the Foundery Society was first established in 1739-
1740, John and Charles Wesley did almost all of the instructional
work. But, as the movement expanded, lay assistants were delegated
oversight in the absence of ordained clergymen. As early as 1744
there were thirty-five lay preachers associated with the Methodist
societies, and many more "local preachers" who gave assistance in
their home societies.[9] The country was divided into "rounds" or
circuits, each of which was the assigned territory of a traveling
preacher, or "helper" as Wesley called them. (From this we get the
term "circuit-rider.") They depended on the societies they visited
for food and lodging, and funds were established to assist their
families. The local preachers stayed in one place and combined
their preaching with their trade. There were seven circuits in
England by 1746 and one hundred fourteen in the British Isles at
the time of Wesley's death.[10]

In addition to the lay assistants, who handled the administration of the societies, Wesley also appointed "stewards" to tend to
the financial aspects of the system, especially the distribution of
goods to the poor, the receipt and recording of funds, and the care
of the meeting facilities.[11] Not only did the stewards perform a necessary financial function; they also provided a vital check-and-bal-

ance system for the group processes of the society. According to items 7 through 10 in the job description, the stewards were to double-check to see that the guidelines laid down in the *Rules* were being followed, and if not, to report to the minister in charge. As in all of Wesley's organizations, those who were appointed to "watch-dog" positions were first to confront those in error in a "spirit of love" before any report of misbehavior was reported. The lay assistants, then, were the spiritual executives of the society; the stewards monitored the inner workings of the group machinery and kept them running smoothly.

It was the Methodist stewards who provided the connecting link between the spiritual and physical ministries of the societies. They were to Methodism what the deacons were to the first century Christian Church: administrators over the temporal affairs of the congregation. Wesley had chosen to aim his ministry toward the poorest and most needy segments of English society, and he recognized in this choice that he was accepting responsibility for tangible physical needs as well as moral and spiritual. Unlike the Religious Societies, in which respectable and comfortably-clad young men discussed interesting points of theology, the Methodist societies were largely composed of the desperately poor, many of them barely clinging to the last threads of existence. To the stewards was given the task of assessing the physical needs of the society members and finding ways to meet them.[12]

Not only were the stewards directed to aid the poor, but even their attitude toward the poor was the subject of a rule: "Give none that ask relief an ill word or ill look. Do not hurt them if you cannot help them." Wesley recognized that a condescending attitude in the distribution of relief goods would jeopardize the good which could be accomplished, not only among the poor, but among those Methodists who were learning by ministering to them. He consciously chose to adapt his lifestyle and language to that of his impoverished clientele, as he perceived Christ had done. He especially warned his helpers about using language that might not be appropriate among unlettered people.[13]

Another set of officers in each society was the trustees, on whom the legal responsibility for Methodist properties rested.[14] The issues handled by the trustees differed widely from place to place because of the diverse circumstances in which Methodist facilities were built. But Wesley conferred upon the trustees a constitutional role which would play a major part in the direction of the societies after his death. He so worded the deeds of each piece of property that the trustees were not only the legal guardians of the buildings but were also responsible for the purity of doctrine preached therein. In the century following the death of its founder, the trustees of Methodism were saddled with the task of determining the orthodoxy of its leaders.

The Methodist societies met for worship and instruction several times each week, but the most widely-known meeting was the Sunday evening meeting. At this time both members and "hearers" were invited to hear a message from Scripture, usually on some practical aspect of Christian lifestyle. These meetings were frequently crowded to the doors, especially if one of the prominent preachers was slated to speak. The effect on the English people can best be illustrated from a census of religious worship conducted by Horace Mann in 1852.[15] On the census Sunday in the three ridings of Yorkshire, 329,572 people attended the Methodist evening services out of a total population of 1,789,147, which is approximately one-sixth. In Cornwall the percentage was even greater, with about one-third—126,401 out of a population of 355,558. The Sunday evening Methodist meeting was a favorite among working-class people, and from the beginning it was a major source of outreach for the Methodist societies.

Wesley had little sympathy for what he called "speechifying," or sermonizing on themes with little practical application.[16] He coached his preachers not only on content and style, but even on the phrases and illustrations they used. He commented:

> I find more profit in sermons on either good tempers or good works, than in what are vulgarly called Gospel sermons.... Let but a pert, self-sufficient animal that has

neither sense nor grace bawl out something about Christ or His blood or justification by faith and his hearers cry out, "What a fine Gospel sermon!"[17]

The content of the Methodist messages bears out Richard Niebuhr's comment that the leaders of the Methodist movement were "impressed not so much by the social evils from which the poor suffered as by the vices to which they had succumbed."[18] Niebuhr's statement seems to be borne out by Robert Wearmouth's extensive studies on the effects of Methodism on the moral climate of England.[19] Wesley had little interest in that kind of preaching which made moral demands on the people or called them to a commitment without following through with specific instruction. The societies, with their ethical and practical teaching, became schools of holy living, complete with provisions for instruction at every level of personal spiritual development.

Another favorite meeting time for the society was early in the morning, before work. These sessions were generally closed to all but society members. They were intended not only to teach the Bible, but also to encourage the working Methodists who were getting ready for life in a difficult working environment. This early morning school for workers did much to civilize the rough laborers; it was a school that developed social responsibility as well as personal character. Wesley waged constant war on sloth and indolence, as well as on sin and spiritual pride. If the phrase about cleanliness being next to godliness didn't originate with him, he certainly advocated that idea. He urged the Methodists:

> Be cleanly! In this let the Methodists take pattern by the Quakers. Avoid all nastiness, dirt, slovenliness, both in your person, clothes, house and all about you.... Mend your clothes, or I shall never expect to see you mend your lives. Let none ever see a ragged Methodist.[20]

He especially enjoyed preaching in the early morning meeting, and the virtues of thrift, industry, and cleanliness were among his favorite subjects. As the people prepared for a busy day, he would admonish them: "Be active, be diligent; avoid all laziness, sloth, indolence. Fly from every degree, every appearance of it: else you will never be more than half a Christian."[21] Even the hymns were geared to encourage discipline and good work habits, as this one which appeared in the first Methodist hymnbook:

Before Their Going to Work

Let us go forth, 'tis God commands;
Let us make haste away;
Offer to Christ our hearts and hands:
We work for Christ to-day.

When He vouchsafes our hands to use,
It makes the labour sweet;
If any now to work refuse,
Let not the sluggard eat.

Who would not do what God ordains,
And promises to bless?
Who would not 'scape the toil and pains
Of sinful idleness?

In vain to Christ the slothful pray:
We have not learn'd Him so:
No; for He calls Himself the Way
And work'd Himself below.

Then let us in His footsteps tread,
And gladly act our part;
On earth employ our hands and head,
But give Him all our heart.[22]

In addition to the regular weekly meetings (early morning preaching and Sunday services) Wesley established several special celebrations, matched to the cultural needs of the people to whom he was ministering. For example, in the rough-and-tumble Kingswood society, the colliers had been accustomed to spending their Saturday nights in revelry at the local ale-house. After they became converts to Methodism, Wesley borrowed a custom from the Moravians to fill the social vacuum on Saturday nights. He instituted the Watchnight, a joyous celebration of Christian life held once a month on Saturday nights and lasting far into the night. These were scheduled as near the full moon as possible so that the participants could travel to and from the Watchnight as easily as possible.

Even though this novelty may have been shocking to the sensibilities of proper English society, Wesley felt that it was a great discovery. It was an effective group tool which could be justified (against any criticisms about its novelty) on the basis of its evident effect and its cultural appropriateness. In its defense, Wesley replied:

> Exceedingly great are the blessings we have found therein; it has generally been an extremely solemn season, when the Word of God sank deep into the hearts even of those who till then knew him not. If it be said, this was owing to the novelty of the thing, (the circumstance which still draws such multitudes together at those seasons), perhaps to the awful stillness of the night, I am not careful to answer in this matter. Be it so: however, the impression then made on many souls has never since been effaced. Now, allowing that God did make use either of the novelty, or by an other indifferent circumstance, in order to bring sinners to repentance, yet they are brought, and herein let us rejoice together. Now, may I not put the case farther yet? If I can probably conjecture, that either by the novelty or this ancient custom, or by an other indifferent circumstance, it is in my power to save a soul from death, and hide a multitude of sins, am I clear before God if I do not? If I do not snatch that brand out of the burning?[23]

A second monthly celebration which was borrowed from the Moravians and adapted to suit the needs of Methodism was the love-feast, a community gathering to affirm the solidarity of the society and to celebrate the progress of its members. A symbolic "meal" of bread and water was followed by witnesses, who one by one gave accounts of their spiritual lessons, achievements, and growth. The focus was clearly on experience—it was not a matter of discussing what should happen, but what was happening in the lives of those who attended. It was a monthly "testimonial dinner," not to eulogize some particular person but to praise God and the institution of Methodism (which they saw as God's instrument).[24]

The setting, officers, literature, special occasions, etc., of the Methodist society mode facilitated its concentration on a cognitive function. Naturally, considering the impassioned preaching and fervent singing, there was an affective dimension of instruction. But the major aim was to present scriptural truth and have it clearly understood.

CLASS MEETING: THE BEHAVIORAL MODE

The class meeting was the most influential instructional unit in Methodism and probably Wesley's greatest contribution to the technology of group experience.[25] Although amazingly simple, it has elicited the praise of educators and religious leaders as a profoundly effective educational tool. Henry Ward Beecher said, "The greatest thing John Wesley ever gave to the world is the Methodist class-meeting."[26] Dwight L. Moody, nineteenth-century revivalist, offered this commendation: "The Methodist class-meetings are the best institutions for training converts the world ever saw."[27] To the class meeting must go much of the credit which many historians have attributed to Methodism[28] for the radical transformation of England's working masses. It was a triumph, not of any human personality, but of an ingenious set of instruments designed for behavioral change.

One of the most striking facts about the class meeting is that it was developed initially as a fund raising scheme in the Bristol Society.[29] Wesley had for some time been frustrated with the lack of close pastoral oversight, especially for those who had recently been converted. He reports,

> But as much as we endeavored to watch over each other, we soon found some that did not live in the gospel. I do not know that any hypocrites were crept in, for indeed there was no temptation; but several grew cold, and gave way to the sins which had long easily beset them. We quickly perceived there were many ill consequences of suffering these to remain among us. It was dangerous to others, inasmuch as all sin is of an infectious nature. It brought such a scandal upon their brethren as exposed them to what was not properly the reproach of Christ. It laid a stumbling-block in the way of others, and caused the truth to be evil spoken of. We groaned under these inconveniences long, before a remedy could be found. The people were scattered so wide in all parts of the town, from Wapping to Westminster, that I could not easily see what the behavior of each person in his own neighborhood was; so that several disorderly walkers did much hurt before I was apprised of it. At length, while we were thinking of quite another thing, we struck upon a method for which we have cause to bless God ever since.[30]

The story of Captain Foy's plan for penny collections is a familiar one to Methodists, for in it lay the solution to Wesley's dilemma:

> I was talking with several of the Society in Bristol (February 15th, 1742) concerning the means of paying the debts there, when one stood up and said: "Let every member of the Society give a penny a week, till all are paid." Another answered: "But many of them are poor, and cannot afford to do it." "Then," said he, "put eleven of the poorest with me, and if they can give nothing, I will give for them as well as for myself; and each of you

call upon eleven of your neighbors weekly; receive what they give, and make up what is wanting." It was done. In awhile some of them informed me they found such and such a one did not live as he ought. It struck me immediately, "This is the thing, the very thing we have wanted so long." I called together all the leaders of the classes (so we used to term them and their companies), and desired that each would make a particular inquiry into the behavior of those whom he saw weekly. They did so. Many disorderly walkers were detected. Some turned from their evil ways, and some were put away from us.[31]

The plan which originated at Bristol was quickly applied to other societies.[32] The class meeting was not to be a voluntary unit adjunct to the society but a subdivision of it. Every Methodist became a member of a class and attended it regularly—or else he or she was no longer a member of the society. The class was to be an intimate group of ten or twelve people who met weekly for personal supervision of their spiritual growth. In April of 1742, the plan was applied to the Foundery Society in London:

(April 25th, 1742) I appointed several earnest and sensible men to meet me, to whom I showed the great difficulty I had long found of knowing the people who desired to be under my care. After much discourse, they all agreed there could be no better way to come to a sure, thorough knowledge of each person than to divide them into classes, like those at Bristol, under the inspection of those in whom I could most confide. This was the origin of our classes at London, for which I can never sufficiently praise God, the unspeakable usefulness of the institution having ever since been more and more manifest.[33]

There were 426 members at that time (plus 201 on trial) in the London society, and they were divided into 65 classes. Eighteen months later, the membership in that one society had grown to 2,200 (December, 1743), all of whom were members of classes.[34]

In 1788, Wesley published a sermon entitled "On God's Vineyard" which included a historical statement about the rise of the class meeting in its wider instructional context. This account not only gives the reader a clearer picture of the beginnings of Methodism, but reveals also Wesley's self-awareness as an instructional innovator. The whole sermon is too lengthy to quote here, but the careful researcher will find it useful and interesting.[35]

When the *Rules for the United Societies* were drawn up in 1744, one brief paragraph became the constitution of the class meeting:

> 3. That it may the more easily be discerned whether they are indeed working out their own salvation, each society is divided into smaller companies called "classes," according to their respective places of abode. There are about twelve persons in every class, one of whom is styled the Leader. It is his business: (1) To see each person in his class once a week at least, in order to inquire how their souls prosper; to advise, reprove, comfort, or exhort, as occasion may require; to receive what they are willing to give toward the relief of the poor; (2) To meet the minister and the stewards of the society once a week; to pay to the stewards what they have received of their several classes in the week preceding; and to show their account of what each person has contributed.[36]

Whereas the society was an instrument for cognitive acquisition, almost to the exclusion of any interpersonal dynamics, the class meeting was a tool for the alteration of behavior, to the virtual exclusion of any data-gathering function. The *Rules* specified the basic process as "inquiry" and the subject matter as "how their souls prospered."[37] There was no room here for lecturing or preaching; the emphasis was clearly on present and personal growth, presided over, not by a professional trainer, but by a fellow seeker.

The particular behaviors which the class meeting was aimed at producing were listed in the *Rules*, which provided a sort of constitution for the class meeting. There were three categories of behaviors specified: (1) prohibitions, or things not to do, (2) exhortations, or positive behaviors, and (3) helpful practices to be maintained, which were known as the "means of grace." These were not conditions of admission, but behavioral targets, as the *Rules* explain:

> 4. There is only one condition preciously required in those who desire admission into these societies,—a desire "to flee the wrath to come, to be saved from their sin": but, wherever this is really fixed in the soul, it will be shown by its fruits. It is therefore expected of all who continue therein, that they should continue to evidence their desire of salvation,

> First, by doing no harm, by *avoiding all evil* in every kind; especially that which is most generally practiced; Such is….

And then are listed various evils to avoid, like "taking of the name of God in vain, drunkenness, buying or selling spirituous liquors, fighting, quarreling, brawling, returning evil for evil" and "borrowing without a probability of paying." Among the positive behaviors listed were "doing good of every possible sort, giving food to the hungry, visiting or helping them that are sick," and living "by all possible diligence and frugality." Finally, among the helpful practices which were encouraged were "the supper of the Lord, family and private prayer, searching the Scriptures" and "fasting or abstinence."

In almost every other function of Methodism, Wesley had insisted on separation of the sexes. Even the Methodist chapels were segregated, men on one side during society meetings, women on the other. But the class meeting was the exception; it was a coeducational experience in small group development. The leadership of the Methodist classes was open to women, and many of the great names of early Methodism were women—Elizabeth Ritchie, Hester Ann Rogers, Agnes Bulmer, Mary Bosanquet—who began as class leaders.[38] Not only were women among the class meeting leaders, but several were preachers as well. As far as the available literature on this period of English history records, this was the only significant position of religious leadership open to women at that time.

Not only were the class meetings mixed groupings according to sex, they were also heterogeneous in terms of age, social standing, and spiritual readiness. In other Methodist groups, especially the bands, there was a closely graded assortment according to the level of spiritual growth. But Wesley visualized the class meeting as the point of entry for most initiates into Methodism, and he wanted the entry group to be a warm fellowship of fellow strugglers, representing a broad cross-section of Methodism. So there were some who were quite mature in their faith and had a good grasp of Methodist doctrine, some who had made a good start on the Christian life and were making progress, and others who were new recruits.

The class meeting provided a forum, available nowhere else in Hanoverian England, for free expression in an accepting environment by people from widely different social backgrounds. Looking back from the perspective of the twentieth century, the Wesleyan class meeting seems to have been the first and probably the most powerful leveling agent which helped to break up the rigid British caste system and provide upward social mobility. Leslie Church, in his analysis of the class rolls of early societies, points out how completely the rich and poor, educated and illiterate, gentlemen and laborers, were united in these classes:

> There is a complete absence of class distinction in these lists. They represent a "family" whose spiritual kinship was recognized by each member. They came together in an intimacy that could not recognize social barriers, and the names of the people who met on perfect equality each appear side by side, whether they are described as

gentlemen or laborers, yeomen or apothecaries. Those who could enter a Methodist society must first abandon all idea of caste.[39]

At first, class meetings met in homes, shops, schoolrooms, attics, even coal-bins—wherever there was room for ten or twelve people to assemble. The chronicles of early Methodism record heroic tales of pious folk, committed to their class, who would undergo great harassment, walk long distances, endure hardship, and put up with bizarre settings in order to "meet in class." However, as Methodist chapels became more available, the classes met in small rooms built for that purpose, arranging their schedules according to the convenience of the members.

The format of the class meeting began with a short hymn (begun promptly at the stated hour) followed by the leader stating the condition of his or her own spiritual life. The leader would then give a short testimonial concerning the previous week's experience, thanking God for progress and honestly sharing any failures, sins, temptations, griefs, or inner battles. In this sense, the leader was "modeling the role" for the others to follow. By following this example, the tenor of the session was controlled and directed. Many of the participants were downtrodden peasants who had been unaccustomed to any expression of their inner feelings and personal experience, so the pace established by the leader was a crucial step in the process. In a classic treatment of the class meeting, John Miley sums up the atmosphere which pervaded the meetings:

> The class meeting was... a means of expression for people who otherwise would not have had the opportunity to speak. It afforded some satisfaction for those who in the polity of the Methodist Church had otherwise no place. The servant girl would follow her mistress in telling the people what God had done for her. The leader of the class might be the manager of the local factory or he might be one of the workingmen engaged there. On the class-leader's book, as members to be vis-

ited, could be found people with every variety of occupation. The social grades were brought to a common level, when each week, the people met together to pray, and praise, and share their experience. The democracy of the class-meeting helped to undermine the Toryism of official Methodism.[40]

The subject matter of a class meeting was personal experience, not doctrinal ideology or biblical information. The only place where conceptual data impinged upon the class process was the struggle which individuals underwent in internalizing or applying or incorporating some biblical ideal into their lives. The collective goal toward which the classes pulled was the attainment of personal holiness, or what Wesley called "perfect love," or the character of Christ. As new converts took up these goals for themselves, they were nurtured in the encouraging context of an affirming group, all of whom were in various stages of the same quest. In 1855, an American class meeting leader named L. Rosser published one of the first definitive works on the class meeting mode, and in it he described the benefits of this learning environment:

In the class-meeting, where religious experience is the only subject of consideration, and the expression of it so plain and simple, it is easy to see how readily an earnest and sincere penitent may obtain instruction and encouragement; as when those who are deeply acquainted with spiritual things refer to the discouragements they encountered, the struggles they endured, the self-denial they had to exercise, the duties they had to perform, and the long dark night of trial they had to pass, before they found forgiveness of sin…. In the suspension of temporal business, in the absence of the world, and in the presence of Christ and his people, the whole soul of the penitent may easily concentrate itself upon being now saved from sin.[41]

Lest it be assumed that the leader was *only* a fellow struggler who got the weekly meeting off to a good start, it needs to be pointed out that there were other dimensions to this role. The leader was a peer, a *primus inter pares* (first among equals), and on the same level with the rest of the class, but he or she was also chosen and appointed for this task in order to assume spiritual oversight and pastoral care for others. The class leader was a sub-pastor in the Methodist organizational hierarchy, and was to carry the concerns of the class through the week.[42]

Not only did class leaders carry the pastoral oversight for their tiny flocks, but it was also made clear throughout Methodism that this position was the first rung of the ladder of leadership. Any future or higher aspirations for leadership roles depended entirely upon faithfulness as a class leader. In this arrangement lies one of the strengths of the Methodist concept of leadership: It took no training or talent to be a class leader; anyone could do it. Being a class leader was in no way related to wealth or education or professional expertise or social standing; it was not an elite position. But, it did demand faithfulness, honesty, and concern for people. Anyone who demonstrated these qualities as a class leader could rise to higher levels of leadership, but without them it was impossible to be a Methodist leader, no matter how educated or wealthy or talented. This one requirement of the Methodist economy was in large part responsible for the practicality and down-to-earth usefulness of Methodism for more than a century.[43]

Another role of the class leader was to establish a climate of acceptance and commitment. As each member reported his or her progress, there was to be an atmosphere of trust and understanding generated by the others and stoked by the leader. As one early class leader, James Field, advised,

> If you would be useful, you must "bear all things." Let nothing offend or move you, though it comes from your dearest friend…. Give none up who have the least spark of spiritual life in them. Remember what they cost Him who hates putting away….[44]

Some critics were alarmed that a group of people could gather for no other reason than to bare their souls and confess their shortcomings—it smacked of narcissism and morbid introspection. But the Methodist class meeting seems to have been far from that. As Leslie Church, in his book, *The Early Methodist People*, explains:

> In the face of these examples… it is ridiculous to dismiss the class-meeting as the product of a passing emotion or to comment, contemptuously, that it was a gathering of neurotics who shut themselves in a selfish circle to practice introspection. Some of the more intimate pages of self-revelation in the personal journals may astonish or shock our modern susceptibilities, but it cannot be too strongly emphasized that the love of self-sacrificial quality which they spoke and sang was, at its best a virile and self-sacrificial quality which sought to give rather than to get.[45]

The members of a class often stayed together for years, cultivating the most intimate and helpful of friendships.[46] In this circle of companionship, it was difficult to be evasive or hypocritical. Deep levels of trust and affection were engendered: an optimum environment for the cultivation of personal character. Hearty thanksgiving and praise to God accompanied and affirmed every step of progress; loving and understanding sympathy and encouragement bolstered personal failures. These Methodists were people who believed that the real joy of human life was spiritual fellowship and moral growth.

> "Nothing," said the high churchman Alexander Knox, "was nearer to New Testament religion than that cheerful piety, habitual pleasure in devotion, and consequent settled self-enjoyment which John Wesley maintained to be the inheritance of the true Christian." In Wesley's view religion began not so much in a sense of past mis-

conduct as in consciousness of present want: his theology dwelt on grace far more as a remedy for corruption and unhappiness, than as a relief from guilt. This cheerful, experimental piety, this active progressive ethic, this synthesis (to use theological terms) of "the Protestant doctrine of grace and the Catholic ethic of holiness" made up Methodism's contribution to the eighteenth century, and was to inspire its work for the new industrial society that lay ahead.[47]

One of the remarkable features of the class meeting format was the realism about human nature that was built into its design. The Puritans had so dreaded human sinfulness that they failed to deal with it objectively; the deists either ignored or glossed over the seriousness of sinful behavior; but Wesley *expected* it and made explicit plans for its treatment in the class meeting. He recognized that those who are seeking to overcome the downward pull of wrong habits will occasionally fall back into them, perhaps often in the beginning. So, he prepared class leaders to expect spiritual "remission" and to lead those who regress back to the right way. A delightful section in the first Methodist hymnbook is entitled "*Hymns Upon Falling into Sin*" and contains appropriate exhortations to the backslider. The next section is apparently intended for celebration of victory, for it is aptly titled "*Hymns Upon Recovering From a Fall*."[48]

In an effort to place the experiential emphasis of the class meeting in historical perspective, it could be generalized that the continental reformers of the sixteenth century had emphasized two great dimensions of church life: the Bible and the sacraments. The next generation of Protestants (seventeenth century) added the dimension of church order and ecclesiastical polity. In the eighteenth century, through the pietists, the Moravians, and the Methodists, the dimension of Christian community comes into the developmental stream. The biblical word which describes this emphasis is *koinonia* and carries the connotation of intimate fellowship and loving concern. The *koinonia* concept was the germinal idea behind the small group experiments which Wesley (and others) undertook in an attempt to experience the inwardness of the true Church, the fellowship of genuine believers.[49]

Wesley recognized the tragic nature of evil and the consequences of sin upon people. Nevertheless, he was a cheerful optimist about the sovereignty and providence of God who could bring even the most recalcitrant sinner under the rehabilitative force of grace. He did not share the pessimism of many of his Protestant forbears, who were quite glum about the chances of human improvement. With a hopeful belief in the perfectibility of man, coupled with a serious determination to save all who could be reached, he mobilized his army of Methodists to "spread scriptural holiness throughout the land" and bring the outcasts back into the redemptive kingdom of God.

> Facing sin and guilt, the Class-Meeting was saved from Pietism and Moralism. Remembering God's forgiveness and His gracious acts, mighty to save, Methodism was kept from resignation and despair. The heart laid bare in the midst of forgiving love—thus does God bring to birth new creatures in Christ.[50]

Wesley's innovations in group processes mark a new turn in religious history, not so much because he introduced new content, but because his methods forced a new orientation in religious knowledge. Like Francis Bacon, Wesley applied the experimental method to Christianity in vivid contrast to the scholastic theologians of the Reformation (and before) with their *a priori* speculations. For Wesley, the locus of activity relevant to the gospel of Christ was the experience or behavior of a person; to most of the Reformers (as McLuhan has pointed out)[51] the locus was in verbal or printed statements—books, pamphlets, creeds, confessions, catechisms, and other doctrinal formulations. If Wesley cannot be known as the "Father of Experiential Religion" as Bacon was "The Father of Modern Science," at least he had the opportunity to apply his theories in practice, a privilege that Bacon never enjoyed:

While Bacon unfolded the true method of science, he did not himself apply his method and make any great discovery or invention…. Wesley applied the experimental method to discover for the Anglo-Saxon peoples the Arminian theology, the "golden mean" between Calvinism upon the one side and Unitarianism on the other. The Wesleyan doctrine of personal freedom and responsibility and the personal consciousness of God's presence accounts in part at least, not only for the spread of Methodism, but for the expansion of the Anglo-Saxon peoples.[52]

Wesley himself made no such historical critique in relation to his near-contemporaries. He saw in the class meeting a return to the societal norms of the first-century Christians. Always fascinated by the functions and practices of the early Church, he kept as his constant reading companions *Cave's* and *Fleury's* works on primitive Christianity. Many feel that he actually had *Cave's* volume in hand when he penned the Rules for the Societies. In the society and its subdivision into classes and bands, he saw the very thing which had been characteristic of earliest Christianity:

Those whom God had sent forth preached the gospel to every creature…. But as soon as any of these were so convinced of the truth as to forsake sin and seek the gospel salvation, they immediately joined them together, took account of their names, advised them to watch over each other, and met these *catechumens* (as they were then called), apart from the great congregation, that they might instruct, exhort, and pray with them and for them according to their several necessities.[53]

The longer Wesley lived, the more he justified his group methods in biblical rather than expedient terms. If he saw the class meeting as "helpful" in his early days, it had become "essential" by the time Methodism was expanding into all corners of the nation. His major concern about any method was whether it worked and produced the desired results—which for the class meeting meant behavioral transformation. In his own evaluation, Wesley seemed to think it *was* working:

> By the blessing of God upon their endeavors to help one another, many found the pearl of great price. Being justified by faith, they had "peace with God, through our Lord Jesus Christ." These felt a more tender affection than before, so those who were partakers of like precious faith; and hence arose such a confidence in each other, that they poured out their souls into each other's bosom.... Indeed they had a great need to do so; for the war was not over, as they had supposed; but they had still to wrestle both with flesh and blood, and with principalities and powers: so that temptations were on every side; and often temptations of such a kind, as they knew not how to speak in class; in which persons of every sort young and old, men and women, sat together.[54]

On one occasion Wesley was asked why the Methodists could not content themselves with preaching and letting God look after the converts instead of going to all the trouble of forming them into societies and classes and bands. Ever pragmatic, Wesley replied, "We have made the trial in various places;... but in all [of them] the seed has fallen by the highwayside. There is scarce any fruit remaining.[55]

The initial and original purpose of the class meeting—to raise money—although overshadowed by the behavioral aim, was never deleted from the format. At each meeting the leader collected each member's penny (more if available, none if too poor) and wrote down the amount in a class-book. The class-books were routinely checked by the stewards and lay assistants. Some of them were simply lists on a blank page; others were a little more elaborate. One class-book carefully kept by Thomas Goulding (1796), the first class leader in Upwell, contained the following preamble:

In opposition to those who call the proud happy, they that fear the Lord assemble themselves together, to speak of the goodness of God, and the Lord hearkeneth and heareth it, and a book of remembrance is written before Him for them that fear the Lord, and that think upon His name. And they shall be mine, saith the Lord of Hosts, in that day when I make up my jewels; and I will spare them, as a man spareth his own son that serveth him. Then will be discerned the difference between the righteous and the wicked, between him that serveth God and him that serveth him not.[56]

One problem which had to be dealt with in the early days of the class meeting was what to do with visitors. Obviously, a stranger or an uncommitted outsider could squelch the spirit of confidentiality and acceptance so essential to the class meeting objectives. It was decided by the Methodist leaders that visitors could attend twice before deciding to join a class. If they chose not to apply for membership, they were from then on excluded from any sessions of the class. Also, in order to protect the fragile environment of the class, every other session was closed to all outsiders.

The society and the class meeting were linked together in three very significant ways. First of all, the class was a subdivision of the society and its leaders were appointed by the leaders of the society and were accountable to them. Secondly, the functions of teaching and behavioral transformation were tied together by the design of the two groups—the class meeting incorporated into the lives of its members what had been taught in the society meetings. Thirdly, active participation in the class meeting was the condition for membership in the society. No one could attend the closed meetings of the society without regular class meeting attendance.

One may ask, "With so many people attending society meetings, how was it possible to know who was or was not a member-in-good-standing of a class?" The answer is very simple: Wesley issued tickets.[57] Every class was visited quarterly by Wesley or one of his assistants and every member was interviewed personally. If the minister determined that the member was faithful to class (missed three or less meetings per quarter), he or she was issued a ticket.[58] Not only did this ensure that all society members would be active in a class; it also provided an inoffensive way to exclude those who were not living by the Rules.

The tickets were originally small cards with the bearer's name, the quarter for which it was issued, and Wesley's signature. These eventually became more ornate, decorated with engraved symbols which were changed with each new quarterly examination. By 1750 Scripture texts began to appear, gradually replacing the symbols or emblems, so that by 1764 the form was standardized.[59] The tickets were an important safeguard for the processes which enabled group development, and Wesley was quick to excise those whose behavior threatened to sabotage the effectiveness of the classes. He was especially wary of any who failed to take the purpose of the class meeting seriously (he called them "disorderly walkers or "triflers"), and he made sure that they did not disrupt or impair or hamper the classes by simply not renewing their tickets.

The purity of the societies and classes was so important to Wesley that he was not the least bit squeamish about putting people out of the group. His *Journal* frequently mentions situations like this:

> (Dec. 9, 1741) God humbled us in the evening by the loss of more than thirty of our little company, whom I was obliged to exclude, as no longer adorning the gospel of Christ. I believe it best to openly declare both their names and the reasons why they were excluded. We all cried unto God that this might be for their edification, and not for destruction.[60]

The same kind of pruning took place in Newcastle the following year (1742), and sixty-four were dropped from membership. In this case Wesley gives in his *Journal* the reasons for their dismissal, illustrating the kind of misbehavior which he felt to be a threat to the group. In the case of 29 members, general "lightness and carelessness" were given as the ground; 17 were dismissed for drunkenness, two for retailing spirituous liquors, four for "railing and evil-speaking," three for "habitual, willful lying," three for quarrelling, two for habitual Sabbath-breaking, two others for cursing and swearing, one for laziness, and another for beating his wife.[61]

The minutes kept in Wesley's *Journal* give an accurate and fascinating account of the man who was perhaps the greatest group organizer of his day. Macaulay's famous statement that Wesley was no less an administrator than Richelieu may be a bit generous,[62] but there is no doubt that he had control of the largest group experiment in England. The fascinating thing is that he was a master of minutia; he knew the importance of small things. His whole endeavor was financed by penny collections. He pored over class lists for hours, writing and recopying lists of names and the brief accounts of their conduct and contributions. He kept an account of every penny he spent and could recite a detailed report of his annual expenditures even years later. He never missed an appointment or preaching engagement, except for the most extreme reasons. By gathering the fine fragments of a massive system into a regimen of accountability, he formed a powerful organization. His control over the entire enterprise was not exercised by bold measures and drastic actions but by the consistent management of minutia. His motto was: "Always in haste; never in a hurry." He said, "I have not time to be in a hurry." One of his assistants, John Fletcher, remarked about his habits:

> Though oppressed with the weight of near seventy years, and the care of near thirty thousand souls, he shames still, by his unabated zeal and immense labors, all the young ministers of England, perhaps of Christendom. He has generally blown the gospel trump, and rode 20 miles, before most of the professors who despise his labors have left their downy pillows. As he begins the day, the week, the year, so he concludes them, still intent upon extensive services for the glory of the Redeemer and the good of souls.[63]

At the center of the transforming methodology of Methodism was the class meeting. It provided the following key elements toward the success of the entire system:

1. It furnished the environment in which cognitive concepts could be experimentally or experientially tested.

2. It served as a purging or pruning instrument to keep "dead wood" out of the society.

3. It was a training ground for leaders.

4. It was a point of entry capable of incorporating large numbers of new people quickly.

5. It financed the movement through penny collections.

6. Its accounting system provided a constant and immediate record of the strength and size of the movement.

7. It forced 100 percent mobilization and participation of the membership.

8. It gave every member a voice in the affairs of Methodism.

9. It allowed people to practice speaking their inner feelings.

10. It provided the milieu for resolving conflicts within the society by immediate face-to-face confrontation.

Wesley himself provided the best evaluation of the class meeting in an article he wrote for the *Arminian Magazine*:

The particular design of the Classes is,—to know who continue as members of the Society; to inspect their outward walking; to inquire into their inward state; to learn what are their trials; and how they fall by or conquer them; to instruct the ignorant in the principles of religion; if need be, to repeat, to explain, or enforce, what has been said in public preaching.

To stir them up to believe, love, obey; and to check the first spark of offense or discord.

To inquire whether they now believe; now enjoy the life of God.

Whether they grow therein, or decay; if they decay what is the cause; and what the cure.

Whether they aim at being wholly devoted to God; or would keep something back.

Whether they take up their cross daily; resist the bent of nature; oppose self-love in all its hidden forms, and discover it, through all its disguises.

Whether they humble themselves in everything. Are willing to be blamed and despised for well-doing. Account it the greatest honor, that Christ appoints them to walk with himself, in the paths that are *His own*. To examine closely whether they are willing to drink of *His cup*, and to be baptized with *His baptism*.

How they conquer self-will, in its spiritual forms; see through all its disguises of themselves; consciousness of their own vileness and nothingness.

How they improve their talents. What zeal they have for doing good, in all they do, or suffer, or to receive from God. Whether they live above it; making Christ their all, and offering up to God nothing for acceptance, but his life and death.

Whether they have a clear, full, abiding conviction, that without inward, complete, universal holiness, no man shall see the Lord. That Christ was sacrificed for us; that we might be a whole burnt sacrifice to God; and that having received the Lord Jesus Christ, will profit us nothing, unless we steadily walk in Him.

I earnestly exhort all leaders of classes and bands, seriously to consider the preceding observations, and put them in execution with all the understanding and courage that God has given them.

J. Wesley [64]

BAND: THE AFFECTIVE MODE

In the Methodist system, the society meetings aimed at cognitive instruction, the class meeting provided an environment for behavioral change, and a third mode—the band—facilitated affective redirection. Unlike the class meeting, it was a homogeneous grouping, not only by sex, but also by age and marital status; the married men met together, the single women, and so on. The bands were voluntary cells of people who professed a clear Christian commitment and who desired to grow in love, holiness, and purity of intention. The group environment was one of ruthless honesty and frank openness, in which its members sought to improve their attitudes, emotions, feelings, intentions, and affections. It could be said metaphorically that the society aimed for the head, the class meeting for the hands, and the band for the heart.

Although the class meeting was the unique, most useful instructional mode within Methodism, the band was Wesley's favorite. It never attained the popularity he hoped for, but it did serve a vital function in the society, at least during his lifetime. The band was the original mode of Methodism, from which the others sprang. It was in Wesley's attempt to perfect the band idea that the other methodologies arose. The central function of the band methodology was what Wesley termed "close conversation," by which he meant soul-searching examination, not so much of behavior and ideas, but of motives and heartfelt impressions.[65] Wesley's personal desire for this kind of intimate interaction appears to have provided the impetus which impelled him to experiment with such diverse schemes as the Holy Club, the Sunday afternoon gatherings in Georgia, the Fetter Lane Society, and finally the Methodist bands. Perhaps there was established in those intimate Thursday evening discourses with his mother a germinal model that attracted him to the Moravians, the little groups founded by de Renty, and the soul-searching books of the mystics. It may have been that same compulsion to find a congenial group of colleagues to whom he could bare his feelings that caught his attention in a little book entitled *A Country Parson's Advice to His Parishioners*.[81] In 1760, in a letter to the *London Magazine*, Wesley credits this little volume for the spark which initiated his experimenting with the band concept:

> About thirty years since I met with a book written in King William's time, called *The Country Parson's Advice to His Parishioners*. There I read these words: "If good men of the Church will unite together in the several parts of the kingdom, disposing themselves into friendly societies, and engaging each other, in their respective combinations, to be helpful to each other in all good Christian ways, it will be the most effectual means for restoring our decaying Christianity to its primitive life and vigor, and the supporting of our tottering and sinking Church."
>
> A few young gentlemen, then at Oxford, approved and followed the advice. They were all zealous Churchmen, and both orthodox and regular to the highest degree. For their exact regularity they were soon nicknamed Methodists....

Nine or ten years after many others "united together in the several parts of the kingdom, engaging, in like manner, to be helpful to each other in all good Christian ways." Their one design was to forward each other in true scriptural Christianity.[67]

The development of Wesley's methodology, as discussed in the biographical section, went through progressive modifications, each of which was later discarded for a better model. Probably the most influential model for the Methodist bands was the Moravian grouping by the same name which Wesley had observed at Herrnhut. He was so awed by the intimacy and depth of relationships experienced by the Moravians that he returned to England and started right away to imitate them. He wrote to the Moravians to tell them about the progress in his bands:

> We are endeavoring here also, by the grace which is given us, to be followers of you, as ye are of Christ. Fourteen were added to us, since our return, so that we now have eight bands of men, consisting of 56 persons; all of whom seek for salvation only in the blood of Christ. As yet we have only two small bands of women; the one of three, the other of five persons. But here are many others who only wait till we have leisure to instruct them, how they may most effectually build up one another in the faith and love of Him who gave himself for them.[68]

The contrast between the ministries of Wesley and George Whitefield was evident in their methodologies before it was noticed in their theologies. Wesley had serious misgivings about "fugitive preachers" who presented a message and called for commitment but did not form the people into groups for follow-up. Initially, when Wesley first launched into field preaching with Whitefield, he believed that band meetings were the right tool by which to incorporate new converts into the church. During this period (1741) he wrote to his brother Charles about establishing bands from Whitefield's converts:

> It is not possible for me to set out yet. I must go round and glean after Mr. Whitefield. I will take care of the books you mention. My *Journal* is not written yet. The bands and society are my first care. The bands are purged; the society is purging; and we continually feel whose hand is in the work.[69]

Although Wesley soon came to realize that an affective instructional mode was not the most appropriate way to follow up field preaching, he was convinced of its supreme value and determined to keep that group near the heart of his ministry. When the class meeting arose in 1742 to supplant the band as the entry group, Wesley elevated the band to a middle level in the system, leaving room at the top for one higher mode. Some Methodist historians contend that, late in life, Whitefield saw the error of his own methodology and lamented that his failure to form bands allowed his efforts to be dissipated.

As has been stated elsewhere, the goal of Methodism which was kept constantly before the people was "to spread scriptural holiness throughout the land." Wesley believed that "holiness" was the grand doctrine of Methodism which God had providentially entrusted to the Methodists. To Wesley, holiness consisted both of outward uprightness or ethical morality and inward purity or "perfect love."[70] His belief in the perfectibility of human nature had both behavioral and affective applications. The design of the Wesleyan program had the goal of holiness in constant focus: The societies proclaimed and explained the doctrine, the class meeting was designed to implement the behavioral quest for holy lifestyle, and the bands facilitated the cultivation of inner purity and the purging of the attitudes. It was an interlocking system, woven around a common theme. Each component depended on the others, and working together to accomplish different facets of the stated goal.

The progression of Methodist converts through successive groups toward a stated goal as their readiness allowed and as mastery was attained at each level reveals a profound knowledge of both human nature and educational philosophy. Since Wesley had no training in group design or any contemporary models to copy, it must be assumed that his understanding was either intuitive or accidental or the result of experimentation. The placement of the behavioral mode *before* the affective mode goes against the grain of widely-accepted thinking about how to effect character improvement. It was the widely-held opinion in Wesley's day (and vestiges of this belief still persist) that human progress begins with the motives or will or "tempers" and extends outward to overt behavior. It came as a revolutionary discovery in 1900 when William James, the father of modern psychology, proclaimed that actions *precede* rather than follow changes in attitude.[71] This was 150 years after Wesley designed a system for correcting behavior *first* (through the class meeting) and feelings or attitudes later through the bands.

As with his other techniques, Wesley's dual standard for excellence was: Is it scriptural, and does it work? Since the band concept was such a shocking novelty to the reserved English temperament, it came under regular and heavy attack. But to all its critics Wesley affirmed that the bands were a renaissance of first-century Christianity. Despite criticism, Wesley established bands on a voluntary basis in every society. There was no requirement that any person belong to a band, but it was advocated strongly in society meetings, and the clear impression was given that sincere seekers after holiness would *want* to be in such a band. The formation of these groups in each society took much the same form as the initial institution of the bands:

> These, therefore, wanted some means of closer union; they wanted to pour out their hearts without reserve, particularly with regard to the sin which did still easily beset them and the temptations which were most apt to prevail over them. And they were the more desirous of this when they observed it was the express advice of an

inspired writer: "Confess your faults one to another, and pray for one another, that ye may be healed."

In compliance with their desire, I divided them into smaller companies; putting the married or single men and married or single women together. The chief rules of these bands (that is: little companies, so that old English word signifies) runs thus:...[72]

By 1744, when the first Methodist Conference was convened, the bands had evolved to the forms which they continued for the next fifty years. The Conference drew up a set of *Rules* specifically for the bands, stating their format, their entry requirements, the questions asked to the applicants, and the instructions for weekly inquiry. Starting with what Wesley conceived as their biblical foundation, the *Rules* laid down the following guidelines:

Rules of the Bands

The design of our meeting is to obey that command of God, "Confess your faults one to another, and pray for one another that ye may be healed" (James 5:16).

To this end, we intend:

1. To meet once a week, at the least.

2. To come punctually at the hour appointed, without some extraordinary reason.

3. To begin (those of us who are present) exactly at the hour, with singing or prayer.

4. To speak each of us in order, freely and plainly, the true state of our souls, with the faults we have committed in thought, word, or deed, and the temptations we

have felt since our last meeting.

5. To end every meeting with prayer suited to the state of each person present.

6. To desire some person among us to speak his own state first, and then to ask the rest, in order, as many and as searching questions as may be, concerning their state, sins, and temptations.[73]

Like the class meeting, each member of a band spoke in turn at each meeting. The difference, however, was in the level of maturity of the participants, the depth of their openness, and the readiness with which they spoke their feelings. In the class meeting, the responsibility was focused on the leader, who was appointed to a pastoral role and who quizzed each member in turn. But in a band meeting, the members took individual initiative to speak their progress toward inward holiness, the leader only serving to start the process.

In order to enable the members to probe the "struggling edge" of their motives and intentions, Wesley proposed a set of "starter questions" to get the process in motion. In our day of sensitivity training, T-groups, and group therapy, the candor and "closeness" of these questions do not seem so improper, but they were perceived as the most objectionable of Wesley's techniques. Even some of his closest friends questioned their use, and his enemies used these as evidence that he was reviving "popery" or the Roman Catholic confessional. Here are the questions, intended to get feelings and attitudes out in the open:

1. What known sins have you committed since our last meeting?

2. What temptations have you met with?

3. How were you delivered?

4. What have you thought, said, or done, of which you doubt whether it be sin or not?

5. Have you nothing you desire to keep secret?[74]

In terms of numbers and popularity, the bands had only limited success. Since they were Wesley's pet group experiment, he advocated their use more persuasively than any other method. In 1768, he directed all his preachers: "As soon as there are four men or women believers in any place, put them into a band. In every place where there are bands, meet them constantly and encourage them to speak without reserve."[75] As late as 1788 he wrote to William Simpson who was then an assistant in the Yarm Circuit: "You should speak to every believer singly concerning meeting in a band. There were always some in Yarm Circuit, though not many. No circuit ever did, or ever will flourish, unless there are bands in the large Societies."[76]

The records of the Foundery Society show that of 2200 members in its society and class meetings, only 639 were involved in the bands, and 300 of these were on trial.[77] Nevertheless, they served an important function in bringing the morale of Methodism under as careful discipline, scrutiny, accountability, and organization as the other components of the system. The beginnings of group therapy are usually traced to the experiments of Dr. J. H. Pratt with his tuberculosis patients in 1905.[78] But here is evidence of an effective and healthy approach to group treatment of emotions and attitudes a century and a half before the movement was underway as a modern science.

Since the environment necessary for "close conversation" was so delicate, no visitors were allowed. Only applicants who had been thoroughly screened, recommended by members of the group who already knew them, and acquainted with the procedures were allowed to join, and then only after a probation period. In order to protect the open discussion in the group, a set of questions was designed to orient applicants to the complete candor which they would experience once in the band.

Considering the historical period from which it comes, it is a masterpiece of group psychology:

> Some of the questions proposed to every one before he is admitted among us may be to this effect:
>
> 1. Have you the forgiveness of sins?
>
> 2. Have you peace with God through our Lord Jesus Christ?
>
> 3. Have you the witness of God's Spirit with your spirit that you are a child of God?
>
> 4. Is the love of God shed abroad in your heart?
>
> 5. Has no sin, inward or outward, dominion over you?
>
> 6. Do you desire to be told of your faults?
>
> 7. Do you desire to be told of all your faults, and that plain and home?
>
> 8. Do you desire that every one of us should tell you, from time to time, whatsoever is in his heart concerning you?
>
> 9. Consider! Do you desire we should tell you whatsoever we think, whatsoever we fear, whatsoever we hear concerning you?
>
> 10. Do you desire that, in doing this, we should come as close as possible; that we should cut to the quick, and search your heart to the bottom?
>
> 11. Is it your desire and design to be, on this and all other occasions, entirely open, so as to speak everything

that is in your heart without exception, without disguise and without reserve?[79]

These questions were not only read to the band member before admission, but there were frequently reiterated in band sessions when the process began to bog down or the participants refused to be completely open. In order for there to be a free and honest discussion of emotions and values, there had to be a very high level of trust and confidence to allow or enable effective treatment.

Wesley's fondness for the band mode no doubt stems from his personal appreciation for the help he had received from "close conversation." He had great regard for those who cared enough about him to ask searching, probing questions concerning his inner life. Even in his later years he happily recalled those deep conversations with Peter Bohler, Christian David at Herrnhut, William Law, and especially his mother Susanna. And, utilitarian that he was, he would not retain a method that was not producing worthwhile effects in the lives of his hearers. He summed up his confidence in the band process with this comment: "I have found by experience that one of these (people) has learned more from one hour's close discourse than ten years' public preaching!"[80]

SELECT SOCIETY: THE TRAINING MODE

In the early years of Methodism, the uppermost group in the instructional hierarchy was the select society. As its name suggests, it was a "select" company of men and women whom Wesley had hand-picked from among the most faithful Methodists. The purpose of this group was to model or exemplify what Methodism was all about, especially the perfecting of the human spirit, and it was to provide a training experience in the doctrines and methods of Methodism. The select society was an elite corps of those enthusiasts who had worked their way up through the ranks of class meeting, society, and band and were considered by both their peers and the leaders to be the standard-bearers of the movement.[81]

Even the high standards of behavior and intimacy of the other modes in the system failed to challenge some of the most zealous converts. The select society provided an environment more suitable for their intensive pursuit of the goals of inward and outward perfection.[82] If their aspirations after the highest ideals of Christian love were thwarted in the lower groups, they found ample room for expression in this highest mode of the system. Membership in the select society was not allowed to be considered as a prize for the attainment of "perfection," not a static plateau at the end of the development process, but rather an intense association to facilitate further striving for growth and Christian service.

Wesley formed the first select society in London in 1742. In a descriptive pamphlet entitled *A Plain Account of the People Called Methodists*, he gave a brief synopsis of its purpose and history:

> VIII. 1. Many of these soon recovered the ground they had lost. Yea, they rose higher than before; being more watchful than ever, and more meek and lowly, as well as stronger in the faith that worketh by love. They now outran the greater part of their brethren, continually walking in the light of God, and having fellowship with the Father, and with his Son Jesus Christ.
>
> 2. I saw it might be useful to give some advices to all those who continued in the light of God's countenance, which the rest of their brethren did not want, and probably could not receive. So I desired a small number of such as appeared to be in this state, to spend an hour with me every Monday morning. My design was, not only to direct them how to press after perfection; to exercise their every grace, and improve every talent they had received; and to incite them to love one another more, and to watch more carefully over each other; but also to have a select company, to whom I might unbosom myself on all occasions, without reserve; and whom I could propose to all their brethren as a pattern of love, of holiness, and of good works.[83]

The members of the select society had not only distinguished themselves as *participants* in other levels of the society, but as leaders. In an early list of those who were members of the first select society at the Foundery, all the names in the group were listed elsewhere as leaders of bands, leaders of classes, or local preachers. This highest mode of the hierarchy was intended to be the capstone of their training experience, so that the membership of the select society provided a constant pool of available and ready leadership for top positions in the system.

As Wesley made clear in his statement of purpose for this group, the inner dynamics of this association were to be a model of how all the modes of Methodism should function: open, honest, committed to each other, caring, and concerned for each other's welfare. Not only were they to be models to "all their brethren as a pattern of love, of holiness, and of good works," but the quality of their group experience should provide a standard of excellence for all the other groups within the system. Rather than explain what kind of group atmosphere he wanted to see in the groups, Wesley had only to point to the environment which was created in the select society as the model case. No doubt the group was not all that Wesley hoped it would be, but his purpose in creating it was to show others the way the process should function.

The select society was dissimilar from the other groups in several ways: It had no "rules," it had no leader, and it had no prescribed format. It was a much more democratic group, with no person officially in charge. Wesley encouraged a freewheeling and open discussion, especially on matters of significance to the direction and policies of Methodism. He welcomed criticism of the system and of his own place in it. He made it clear that in this context, the participants would hammer out strategy for the societies and have a major voice in the decision-making process.[84] Although the members of the select society were in training in a sense, they were learning to lead by making decisions and establishing policies and sharpening doctrine.

Although there were no rules for this mode, there were three "Directions," two of which were guarantees of the unity of the group: Everything said was in absolute confidence, and in all "indifferent matters" or inconsequential opinions the members would agree to submit to and abide by the arbitration of the senior minister. The third direction bore a theme by now common to all Methodist groups: Everyone would contribute what they could to the common stock.

Wesley described the open atmosphere as follows:

4. Every one here has an equal liberty of speaking, there being none greater or less than another. I could say freely to these, when they were met together, "Ye may all prophesy one by one," (taking that word in its lowest sense), "that all may learn, and all may be comforted." And I often found the advantage of such a free conversation, and that "in the multitude of counselors there is safety." Any who is inclined so to do is likewise encouraged to pour out his soul to God. And here especially we have found, that "the effectual fervent prayer of a righteous man availeth much."[85]

Not only did the select society have a special purpose for the lay participants, it was also a place of psychological refuge for Wesley himself. He needed a "home base," an intimate fellowship of like-minded companions to share his failures and defeats, progress and victories, frustrations and hopes. He needed a forum of friends in which to work out the implications of his own personal quest for holiness, a strategy group who could sharpen the focus of his own thinking. He feared that level of leadership which creates its own pedestal, alienating the leader from his colleagues and causing them to fear being frank and open with him. Wesley refused to be adulated by his followers and to be told only what he wanted to hear. He demanded the truth, not only about the societies, but especially about himself. In the select society he found that ultimate executive committee, a company of peers who were totally committed to each other, sharing a common goal, and were willing to "speak the truth in love."

Throughout the pages of Wesley's *Journal* we get only occasional glimpses into the select societies. We do know that in 1745, there were twenty-five men in the select society at London, and that in some instances women were also among the group.[86] Wesley speaks with particular appreciation, for example, of a certain Negro woman who ministered to him in the select society in Whitehaven in 1780.[87] Perhaps there is so little record because the deliberations of the select society were to be kept within the group. There was no provision for any kind of accounting as there was in other groups. Also, since the select society was not a mode which continued after Wesley's death, little attention has been paid to its history.[88]

Penitent Bands: The Rehabilitative Mode

One final group in Wesley's system was specially designed for those who lacked the will power or personal discipline to live up to the behavioral demands of the class meeting but still had a desire to overcome their personal problems. Since the target population of the Methodist system was what many considered "the dregs of English society," the instructional hierarchy of groups needed some alternative route for those with serious social dysfunctions.[89] For these, Wesley designed an entirely different kind of group: the penitent band.

> VII. 1. And yet while most of these who were thus intimately joined together, went on daily from faith to faith; some fell from the faith, either all at once, by falling into known, willful sin; or gradually, and almost insensibly, by giving way in what they called little things; by sins of omission, by yielding to heart-sins, or by not watching unto prayer. The exhortations and prayers used among the believers did no longer profit these. They wanted advice and instructions suited to their case; which as soon as I observed, I separated them from the rest, and desired them to meet me apart on Saturday evenings.[90]

The primary goal of the penitent band was to restore its members to the mainstream of the society and its regular channels of growth. Apparently they were successful in a number of cases. The penitents met on Saturday nights (even the scheduling was designed to keep them out of their old haunts), and the minister in charge selected whatever measures were necessary to deal with their moral problems, primarily alcoholism. In fact, this group, in its rigorous format and stringent means for personal reform, is very similar to Alcoholics Anonymous.

Wesley described the rigorous format of the penitent band as follows:

> 2. At this hour, all the hymns, exhortations, and prayers are adapted to their circumstances; being wholly suited to those who did see God, but have now lost sight of the light of his countenance; and who mourn after him, and refuse to be comforted till they know he has healed their backsliding.

> 3. By applying both the threats and promises of God to these real, not nominal, penitents, and by crying to God in their behalf, we endeavored to bring them back to the great "Shepherd and Bishop of their souls;" not by any of the fopperies of the Roman Church, although, in some measure, countenanced by antiquity. In prescribing hair-shirts, and bodily austerities, we durst not follow even the ancient Church; although we had unawares, both in dividing the believers, from the rest of the society, and in separating the penitents from them, and appointing a peculiar service for them.[91]

The actual format and techniques of the penitent band are largely lost to us, but we do know that they continued to meet in several places for a number of years. The necessity of a rehabilitative mode in any system of human development is evident by its many successors today.

CHAPTER FOUR

Why Was Wesley's System So Effective?

As has been demonstrated in the previous chapters, John Wesley's instructional system arose within the context of the cultural and historical circumstances of eighteenth-century England. His methodology was, in part, the product of his response to personal and social conditions in that day. He was no ivory-tower theorist; he worked with the common stuff of public ministry and formulated his policies in the midst of hectic situations. Therefore, there is a sense in which his system cannot be understood or even analyzed apart from the historical context in which he lived and worked. However, in the design of Wesley's program, there are methodological principles which may be extracted, not only for analysis, but also for application in other instructional settings.

The uniqueness of Wesley's system may be displayed and examined on at least four different levels. The first and foundational level is that set of underlying principles of which the remainder of the system is the logical expression. The second level has to do with those particular strategies of group interaction which coalesce into an instructional methodology. The third level relates to the principles of leadership which gave impetus to the Methodist movement. A final analysis may be made of those supplementary instructional aids which the Methodists employed that were neither unique nor essential to the system.

The Foundation Principles

John Wesley's educational enterprise was at its core a religious quest; therefore, its underlying presuppositions are cast in spiritual terms rather than technical or philosophical terms. Although he was aware of contemporary educational theorists—he admired Locke and despised Rousseau[1]—his rationale for group instruction was shaped by spiritual, not secular, considerations. However, despite the explicitly religious context, Wesley's methodology can be studied in the same manner as any other system, especially those which also purport to inculcate an ideology. With a couple of major exceptions, Wesley's key educational ideals address those issues common to any educational philosophy: What is the nature of humanity? How do people learn? What is the nature of their learning environment? What is the effect of social setting on learning? What factors motivate people to change? In order to understand Wesley, it is also necessary to ask: What is humanity's relationship to God, and what is the nature and function of the Church?

Eight major concepts form the bulwark of Wesley's educational philosophy. These will be presented first by listing them as a group, then giving a brief description and/or clarification of each:

1. Human nature is perfectible by God's grace.

2. Learning comes by doing the will of God.

3. Mankind's nature is perfected by participation in groups, not by acting as isolated individuals.

4. The spirit and practice of primitive Christianity can and must be recaptured.

5. Human progress will occur if people will participate in "the means of grace."

6. The gospel must be presented to the poor.

7. Social evil is not to be "resisted," but overcome with good.

8. The primary function of spiritual/educational leadership is to equip others to lead and minister, not to perform the ministry personally.

1. *Human nature is perfectible by God's grace.*

A major theme of Wesley's ideological system was what he called "holiness," "perfect love," "Christian perfection," or "entire sanctification." By this he meant that all people could, and should, reach toward moral perfection and expect to attain it. One early class meeting leader summarized Wesley's position this way:

> The doctrine of experimental holiness has been taken as distinctive of Methodism, under the term "Christian perfection," in accordance with an earnestly and repeatedly-expressed desire for the Corinthian believers, "and this we also wish, even your perfection;" your perfect restoration to harmony as a church as the result of your individual purity and mature conformity to Christ. This perfection as believed in by the Methodists is not absolute perfection, that belongs to God only, but Christian perfection—full salvation from sin. It is not such a perfection as places the Christian beyond the possibility of mistake, or misunderstanding, or misjudgment, or forgetfulness, or any mere infirmity of our mortal nature which may bring trials after it, though not necessarily involving condemnation; but it is perfect sincerity, guilelessness of soul, after the example of him whom the Heart Searcher called "an Israelite indeed, in whom is no guile." No guile as to God, always willing to be open to His view: no guile as to our neighbour, a conscious freedom from all evil, in thought, word, or deed, towards him: no guile as to self, no wish to think of oneself other than God thinks. This perfection is not one which renders the atonement no longer necessary,... but it is rather the perfection of faith....[2]

Wesley believed that people, without the aid of God's grace and in the context of a contaminated society, could improve neither their moral condition nor their standing with God. However, if any individual would respond to God in faith, repent of rebellion against God, and live in obedience to God's commands, he or she would not only find eternal salvation but be on the track toward moral purity. Wesley recognized the uniqueness of this position in regard to the perfectibility of human nature, and he considered it the major thrust of the Methodist message. "This doctrine," said he, "is the grand depositum which God has lodged with the people called Methodists; and for the sake of propagating this chiefly He appeared to have raised us up."[3] When the preachers asked Wesley what should be done to reform and/or revive the Church, Wesley replied, "Strongly and explicitly exhort all believers to go on to perfection."[4] He passionately believed that God could, and would, purify people's hearts so that they would attain Christlike character, and this theme became the overarching goal of the entire movement. It was everywhere displayed and proclaimed, so that no one was in doubt about what Methodism was trying to accomplish—"to spread scriptural holiness throughout the land."

The perfectibility or even changeability of human nature was not a popular idea in the eighteenth century. Like the Puritans a generation earlier, many Anglicans and Dissenters alike believed in the doctrine of "predestination," not only that every person was either predetermined to salvation or damnation, but also that human nature was immutable. Many studies have been written on the influence of John Calvin's thought on post-Reformation Europe and colonial America, since Calvin was the popularizer and leading proponent of deterministic anthropology.[5] Wesley viewed Calvinism, with its fatalistic outlook on humanity, as the antithesis of his own system. When asked, "What is the direct antidote to Methodism, the doctrine of holiness?" Wesley replied:

Calvinism: all the devices of Satan, for these fifty years, have done far less toward stopping this work of God than that single doctrine. It strikes at the root of salvation from sin previous to glory, putting the matter on quite another issue…. Be diligent to prevent them and to guard those tender minds against the predestinarian poison…. Very frequently, both in public and in private, advise our people not to hear them. Make it a matter of constant and earnest prayer that God would stop the plague.[6]

Wesley's optimism about human potential was expressed in the total Methodist system of group instruction. The commitment to a supreme purpose which had both behavioral and affective goals kept Methodism from morbid introspection. Because of the goal-orientation and the hope of attaining it, the groups were kept from stagnation. The idea that human nature could improve with proper care and discipline was an essential plank in the Wesleyan instructional platform.

2. *Learning comes by doing the will of God.*
Very much like the progressive educators of the twentieth century, Wesley believed that learning comes through experience. Methodism was an experiential system, as opposed to those which primarily emphasized either cognitive acquisition or belief in propositional truth. The difference between the meetings of the Methodists and other religious groups of their day was that many church leaders were telling people what they ought to do, but the Methodists were telling each other what they *were* doing. When Methodists met with their classes or bands, they shared up-to-date accounts of their experiences. There was no discussion allowed in the whole system which was theoretical or hypothetical or speculative; if it was not practical, it was not proclaimed.

Alfred North Whitehead has given a definition of experience which comes close to the Methodist objective: "Experience is first of all doing something; then doing something that makes a difference; and finally knowing what difference it makes."[7] Wesley would have agreed to that basis of learning except for one great exception: He advocated experience which resulted from obedience to the

Word of God. The Bible was the starting point from which all experience was to originate and against which all experience was to be judged. The whole program of Methodism was a behavioral struggle; it was not so much what one believed, but something one did, that made him or her a Methodist.

Wesley anchored his behavior-shaping ministry in the Sermon on The Mount, in which Christ presented the behavioral norms for his disciples to follow. The capstone of that sermon is the parable of the wise man who built his house on the rock and the fool who built on the sand. The wise man, Jesus said, was the one who heard his words *and did them,*[8] while the fool was only a hearer.[9] Saint James added the injunction, "Be doers of the Word; not hearers only."[10] And Wesley follows in the same tradition with a central focus on *doing.* Methodism was not just a message to be proclaimed, it was a lifestyle to be embodied.

3. *Human nature is perfected by participation in groups, not by acting as isolated individuals.*

Wesley was convinced that learning is expedited by group interaction, whether the content of that learning is behavioral transformation, redirection of attitudes and motives, cognitive data-gathering, strategic training, or social rehabilitation. It seems that he responded to every instructional need he met by establishing a group, some kind of group. He felt that his own personal growth was largely due to participation in group experiences, and he advocated them for others. Depending on the educational goal to be accomplished, the size and format of his groups varied, but there was always the people-to-people element in his solution to human problems and development.

Probably the most succinct statement of Wesley's belief in human association for learning is found in the "Preface to the 1739 Methodist Hymnbook." (See Appendix C.) Not only does he list the advantages and scriptural basis for the "social" or group learning context, but he sharply condemns those systems which isolate learners from their peers. He especially felt that cognitive presentation which was not followed through with behavioral application was not only useless, but destructive, as in this quote:

> That part of our economy, the private weekly meetings
> for prayer, examination, and particular exhortation, has
> been the greatest means of deepening and confirming
> every blessing that was received by the word preached,
> and of diffusing it to others, who could not attend the
> public ministry; whereas without this religious connec-
> tion and intercourse, the most ardent attempts by mere
> preaching have proved of no lasting use.[11]

There are some who have seen in the disciplinary and utopian
scheme of Methodism an attempt to revive the rigor and spirit of
monasticism, which may be an adequate comparison as long as the
individualism of the monastic experience is not included in the
similarity. Wesley's often-quoted aphorism, "There is no holiness
but social holiness"[12] sums up his belief that Christian perfection is
a group experience rather than a solitary quest.

4. *The spirit and practice of primitive Christianity can and must
be recaptured.*

Nearly every utopian thinker has urged a return to the "good
old days" before the evils of the present system fouled the human
community. Marx wished for a return to the simplistic, classless
communalism of precapitalistic Europe, Rousseau yearned for the
Eden of the noble savage, and Wesley attempted to return to the
uncluttered religion of the first-century Christians. This drive to
regain the pristine purity of the early Church led him to jettison
much of the cultural baggage which he saw as humanly created
accretions upon the lifestyle instituted in the Bible. He did not view
church history as the progressive unfolding of God's plan, but
rather as deviations from the correct model of Christianity followed by occasional returns to it. He looked upon his own movement as a retrogression toward primitive Church life, instead of a
progressive movement coming out of Anglicanism. His search was
for the spirit and practice of the early Christians, and he felt that he

found it in the intimate fellowship of sincere believers. Here is the true Church: not in some particular form of church government, not in some creed, not in any ritual or custom, but in the pure atmosphere of an intensive group.

Whatever Wesley's motivations in staking his authority on a quest for biblical simplicity, it had a profound effect in the minds of his adherents. The belief that this movement had its origin in authentic New Testament norms rather than in human expedience gave it tremendous credibility in their eyes. It also increased the hostility of its critics; which, in turn, further strengthened and enhanced its significance to the faithful. Every comparison Wesley made between Methodism and the early Church (and there were many), heightened the sacredness of the movement and strengthened its normative power.

Wesley not only believed that a return to the practices of the early Church was a possibility, but that it was a perennial necessity to return to that pattern. This deliberate attempt to simplify theology and restore the "faith once delivered to the saints" probably did much to sweep Methodism from an obscure little sect to a nationwide mass movement. As the church historian Harnack points out, "Every great religious movement is characterized by a return to simplicity in doctrine."[13] The personal zeal for primitive Christianity enabled Wesley to pare much of the excess verbiage from the current theology and refine it into simple formulae palatable to common believers.

5. *Human progress will occur if people will participate in "the means of grace."*

John Wesley had great confidence in those activities of the Church which were instituted to promote personal spiritual growth: communion, baptism, Bible reading, prayer, preaching, and confession. To this list of "instituted means" Wesley added his own list of "prudential means" which were primarily group experiences like the class meeting and the band. He believed that these instruments, if people would only participate or "partake" of them, would almost guarantee progressive growth.[14] To Wesley, these activities were the mechanism which put people in touch with the dynamic power of God's grace. As an orthodox Anglican, he always affirmed that God's grace was the agent of change, but the activities of devotion enabled that grace to become effective in people's lives.

One of the ways this foundational principle affected the Methodist system was that active participation was the only real requirement for membership, both initial and continuing. Wesley had such faith that the system would achieve the desired results that he felt no need for other controls. The groups would maintain their own controls by means of their built-in mechanisms as long as they were filled by willing and serious participants. The two major reasons for which members were expelled from the system were (1) unfaithfulness to their groups and (2) dysfunctional behavior which threatened the processes of the system.

6. *The gospel must be presented to the poor.*

It was no accident that Methodism was initially a lower echelon movement; it was a matter of religious conviction and philosophy. In his attempt to follow the guidelines of the Bible, Wesley imitated Christ and the apostles in beaming the gospel message downward toward the most needy rungs of the social ladder. He developed a keen sense of mission to aid the disadvantaged, quoting as his rationale these words of Christ: "Blessed are the poor in spirit, for theirs is the kingdom of heaven" (Matthew 5: 3).

There is no evidence in Wesley's writings to indicate that he was aware of the potential movements among the poor. He was intent on reaching as many people as he could, but he apparently did not have a conscious design to launch a nationwide spiritual awakening, even though he deliberately selected that segment of the social order most likely to generate a demographic upheaval. Recent research has confirmed that religious renewal, especially on a national basis, rarely, if ever, descends from the top of the social system to the masses at the bottom.[15] It seems that Wesley's reason for aiming his approach to the poor was simply to follow biblical precedent, but whatever the motivation, he hit upon a key principle of mass movements. Eric Hoffer in his study of mass movements entitled *The True Believer* points out that it is not only the poor, but a certain type of poverty, which breeds mass religious or political movements.[16] Hoffer distinguishes between several types of poor—the abject poor, the unified poor, the new poor, the creative poor—and identifies exactly the social condition in which Methodism worked as the ideal milieu for cataclysmic upheaval.

The principle of ministering to the poor was evident in the Methodist system at every turn. The vocabulary, instructional setting, leadership patterns, and even the emphasis on group learning were concessions and adjustments to a poor and poorly-educated audience. The choice of this particular social element as Methodism's exclusive clientele influenced the whole structure and direction of the system. The emphasis on group learning is particularly appropriate to working-class audiences, as opposed to that individual emphasis which pervades the methodologies designed for the socially and intellectually well-to-do. In his *Armies of the Night* Norman Mailer paints the contrast between the association patterns of the working class and the educated elite:

[The upper-middle class was alienated from] that sense of élan, of morale, for *buddies are the manna* of the working class.... The working class is loyal to friends, not ideas.[17]

7. Social evil is not to be "resisted," but overcome with good.

Movements for social reform have historically taken four major approaches to social ills: (1) stay within the structures of society which promote or allow evil and work to change them, (2) go outside the traditional structures and model an alternative, (3) stand outside the system and call for the change or destruction of its oppressive structures (the prophetic approach), or (4) change the system by changing the individuals within it. Of these four, Wesley adhered to the fourth alternative as the proper and most effective way to address the ills of society. He was a staunch Tory by political persuasion and opposed revolution for any reason. Although he later made concessions to its existence, he abhorred the American revolution and exerted his energies against it. He advocated peaceful and orderly change through proper channels and through instruction and persuasion of people involved in unlawful or immoral practices.

The behavioral goals outlined for the class meeting included the elimination of several social problems: alcoholism, smuggling, violence, deception in selling, and pawnbrokering. Probably the most widespread and difficult social malady of the eighteenth century was alcoholism, which had become almost epidemic. Rather than launch a Carrie Nation-like campaign against saloons and grogshops, Wesley chose rather to (1) rehabilitate the alcoholic through group therapy, (2) educate individuals through the society against indulgence, and (3) use social pressure within the Methodist groups to discourage the use of liquor.

Richard Niebuhr was probably correct in saying that Wesley attacked personal vices rather than social systems,[18] although he did rally the Methodist masses behind the drive to abolish slavery. There has been some criticism by contemporary social analysts that Wesley was less than fully Christian for not making a frontal attack on the institutions of English society which oppressed and exploited the working classes. However, it was from the words of Christ and Saint Paul that Wesley drew his formula for redeeming the victims of social injustice: "Resist not evil;[19] overcome evil with good."[20] In his typical approach to a poverty-stricken and vice-ridden situation, Wesley preached a sermon on God's grace, called those who were serious to join a group, and established a society there. The design of the Methodist system, built around the concept of conquering evil with good, gave it an aggressive stance toward social problems. Since moral improvement was Methodism's stock-in-trade, oppressed and destitute people were its raw material.

8. The primary function of spiritual/educational leadership is to equip others to lead and minister, not to perform the ministry personally.

In Wesley's day (and in many places still today) the function of ministry within a congregation was vested in one professional clergyman. He was paid and trained to be the "minister" and there were ecclesiastical rules to keep untrained laymen from usurping his role. Although Martin Luther had boldly proclaimed the "priesthood of all believers" in the sixteenth century, that ideal had never become a reality even in the Protestant Church. Wesley, however, so mobilized the entire Methodist membership that nearly every member had some share in the ministry of the congregation. Within the hierarchy of Methodist groups, there were dozens of official positions—stewards, class-leaders, band leaders, exhorters, trustees, sick-visitors, helpers, preachers, booksellers—so that the ministry was parceled out to the entire body of believers, not just the chosen elite. This sharing of the leadership role called for a totally different approach to spiritual and educational leadership. Rather than performing the "ministry" themselves, the leaders' main task was the training or equipping of the leaders at lower levels. This concept had a precedent in Scripture when Saint Paul instructed the church at Ephesus: "And He [God] gave some as apostles, and some as evangelists, and some as prophets, and some as pastors and teachers, for the equipping of the saints for the work of ministry to the building up of the body of Christ."[21] This concept of leadership alone was revolutionary enough to set Methodism apart from other sects which practiced a one-person ministry. Naturally, it roused the ire of those clergymen whose position might be threatened by such a sharing of the ministerial function, but it enabled thousands of common Christians to have a direct role in the shaping of their own church, and ultimately of the direction of the nation.

These eight cardinal principles form a strong supportive base for the group technology of Methodism. Far from being a random discovery, Wesley's system was the logical outworking of a set of deep convictions. The methods he used were gleaned from a wide variety of sources, but he was not just a pragmatic eclectic who experimented with whatever was expedient. Rather, his educational concepts enabled him to choose appropriate instructional strategies that would match the philosophical base. It was this underlying set of principles which enabled him to see the value of methods others had overlooked or discarded. This is the reason, for example, that he so readily seized upon Captain Foy's class meeting discovery; it matched the principles he already believed. Therefore, his educational system can be analyzed at its foundational level on these eight basic beliefs. This forms a basis of comparison then with other systems.

GROUP STRATEGIES

The Wesleyan instructional system is a synthesis of effective group methods drawn from a wide range of sources. Some of the methods were his own inventions, some he borrowed from others (either intact or modified), and still others arose as by-products of other projects. His borrowing capacity was not unlike the imitativeness of other mass movements described by Eric Hoffer:

> When an active mass movement displays originality, it is usually an originality of application and of scale. The principles, methods, techniques, etcetera which a mass movement applies and exploits are usually the product of a creativeness which was or still is active outside the sphere of the movement. All active mass movements have that unabashed imitativeness which we have come to associate with the Japanese. Even in the field of propaganda the Nazis and the Communists imitate more than they originate.[22]

The ingredients Wesley put together to mobilize and train the English poor may lack the sophistication of a modern instructional system. Nevertheless, there is a unity to his system and a symmetry of design which kept the disparate elements in balance. The major methodological components of Wesley's technology are listed below, followed by a brief description and/or clarification of each:

1. A hierarchy of interlocking groups.

2. The point of entry to the system is behavioral change, followed by affective, aspirational, and rehabilitative functions.

3. Constitutional authority.

4. Groups graded by readiness of participants.

5. Total participation and mobilization.

6. Instrumented group activities.

7. Exclusion (by ticket) for noncompliance.

8. Individualized care.

9. Multiple accountability.

10. Separation of cognitive, affective, and behavioral functions.

1. A hierarchy of interlocking groups.

Each instructional grouping within the Wesleyan system was related to the ones above and below it in the hierarchy, although their functions were different. The leading members of one group were almost always participants in the next group up the ladder. For example, the leader of a class was almost always a member of one of the bands, whose leader was, in turn, automatically a member of the select society. The ladder continues upward into the administrative system: The ranking member of the local select society was a local preacher, and as such was a member of the circuit, which was presided over by an assistant, and so on up. The entire local system was encased in the encompassing jurisdiction of the society, which has been described as the didactic mode of the overall system. The progression which an individual followed through the system was not only an advancement in degree of participation, but also a change of instructional purposes, beginning with behavior.

2. *The point of entry into the system is behavioral change, followed by affective, aspirational, and rehabilitative functions.*

The process of becoming a Methodist started with doing what a Methodist does, enabled and enforced by the techniques for behavioral change built into the class meeting mode. The behaviors to be acquired were clearly defined in the *Rules*, and their frequent repetition aided the new converts in their first learning task: to act like a Methodist. In Wesley's system, doing the will of God, even on the most rudimentary level, always precedes cognitive "knowing." True knowledge, for a Methodist, was the natural outgrowth of proper practice; not vice versa.

Upon the basis of experience, other areas of a new Methodist's personality were explored. If zeal carried one past the behavioral level, higher groups were found which could relate to the perfecting of attitudes, social skills, doctrinal understanding, and leadership abilities. But every new bit of information was referred to the behavioral application. Regardless of how far into the system one went, a Methodist never outgrew the need (or requirement) for behavioral change through the class meeting.

3. *Constitutional authority.*

The locus of authority in the Methodist groups was shifted, very wisely, from Wesley himself to a set of group charters, or *Rules*. These *Rules*, or published statements of purpose and procedure, became the standard against which all policies and actions were measured. Every group had its own set of *Rules*, and frequent reading of these documents was designed to preserve the original intention of the group.

One great advantage of constitutional authority as opposed to authority vested in a leader or the majority of a group is that its impersonal nature is no threat to the feelings of the members. For example, one of the questions prescribed for use in the bands was, "What temptations have you met?" If this question had originated with some member, even the leader of the group, the person being questioned might well respond, "Who are you to be asking me about my temptations?" However, since it was not a person or group of people asking, but an impersonal charter to which all had willingly subscribed, the threat level was decreased. The public nature of the group constitutions enabled deep probing into sensitive areas without unnecessary personal pressure. And, because all were under the same authority, there was equality and unity that might have been impossible had authority rested on any one individual.

4. *Groups graded by readiness.*

One educational strategy that was no accident for Wesley was the placement of people into separate groupings according to their readiness. He knew the dangers of too wide an interest spread within any one group, so he kept constant check on every member's readiness level. There were several methods for determining whether or not a member was ready for group participation: (1) the class-leaders gave a monthly report on each member's progress to the preacher in his or her society, (2) each class member was interviewed quarterly by the senior minister and a record was made of the member's spiritual condition, and (3) entry questions for the bands enabled the applicant to make a self-evaluation of his or her own preparedness to participate. Once the groupings had been closely-graded according to readiness levels, the content and methods could be matched to suit a fairly homogeneous membership.

5. *Total participation and mobilization.*

The Methodist system of intensive groups was fine for gregarious people, but it was no place for a recluse or loner. It seems incredible, but *every* Methodist spoke at *every* meeting *every* week (except for society meetings). There was no allowance for mere listeners or watchers. The success of the entire system hinged on the assumption that everyone would participate fully.

Later, in the nineteenth century, Sunday evening meetings were opened to those who were "hearers only," and their attendance was recorded under that rubric.[23] By the time the requirement of participation had been dropped as a condition for membership, the entire Methodist group system had crumbled and Methodism became just another religious denomination with no particular methodological distinction.

6. Instrumented group activities.

In the past quarter century, a number of discoveries have been made in the field of group dynamics. "Instruments" or published guidelines have been produced to lead groups through certain processes. There are "instruments" sold on the market to enhance teamwork, develop intimacy, practice group skills, improve listening ability, and many other group activities. The design and use of prepared materials for group guidance is becoming a science in itself.

Of the groups which Wesley designed, two would be considered "instrumented groups": the class meeting and the band. In these modes, a prepared list of questions provided the external impetus to start the interactive process and keep it going. This technique was never really developed beyond the initial stage, and after Wesley's death the questions soon dropped from use.

7. Exclusion (by ticket) for noncompliance.

There was a clear separation in the Methodist system between the "ins" and the "outs." Those who willingly and actively participated in the group functions were in, those who refused to cooperate were out. There was no "occasional" participation. The solidarity of the smaller units of the system was protected by not allowing any casual attendance. Wesley continually had to goad some of his more softhearted preachers to keep the standards of admission on the basis of participation alone. Also, some of the societies which were raising money for various projects had difficulty excluding those who were large contributors, even though their attendance record was spotty. This preferential treatment of the rich especially rankled Wesley, and at several of the Methodist Conferences he threatened to remove any preacher found guilty.

The idea of tickets allowed the Methodist leaders to maintain the integrity of the groups while keeping conflict to a minimum. Naturally there were those who protested loudly about being put out of the society, but their exclusion was deemed a necessary safe-guard and the tickets a convenient restraint.

8. *Individualized care.*

Every Methodist was under someone else's direct and immediate supervision. There was a constant emphasis on "bearing one another's burdens," so that not even the slightest affliction went unnoticed. As one disgruntled Anglican clergyman complained,

> The discipline of the Methodists is such an artful and well-linked chain of dependence that every man is either an office bearer, or under the immediate superintendence of some other person of his own rank and near his own size of understanding. The framers of the Church of England contemplated no such state of things as this. They provide one guide to one flock and expected that they should look to him alone. Accordingly the parish minister now stands single against a host of bands, classes, and nameless authorities all acting with the compact and uniform force produced by combination.[24]

9. *Multiple accountability.*

The group processes of Methodism were under a simple but thorough system of constant surveillance. Just as a scientist can monitor a complicated and vast system by watching a panel of gauges, dials, and meters, so the Methodist local preacher could monitor the society by examining the class-books and records that were regularly submitted. Near the end of his life, Wesley could claim that he "knew" all of the 30,000 people in his societies by name and what was the condition of their spiritual life. He did have available to him the exact and multiple record of all the transactions of the societies, and he made it his business to know the state of every facet of the system. The record-keeping process was an essential ingredient to the proper functioning of the group system, and Wesley kept it well-oiled.

10. *Separation of cognitive, affective, and behavior functions.*

One strategy which greatly enhanced the success of the Methodist system was the clear focus in each instructional mode on only one type of objective. Wesley avoided the temptation to try to accomplish too many purposes in any level of instruction. He carefully kept the various functions of his movement separate by limiting each group level to one major function: class meetings to alter behavior, societies to present information, bands to perfect "affections," and so on. The reason this is such an advantage is that it allowed each function to be individually tailored and monitored. For example, if there was a problem in a particular society, it was a fairly simple procedure to locate the flaw in the system and correct it without disrupting the whole program.

This nexus of compatible strategies facilitated both effective instruction and ready supervision. The components seemed to work harmoniously despite the fact that they were applied under a fairly wide range of cultural settings.

LEADERSHIP PRINCIPLES

One level at which the Methodist system may be evaluated relates to its principles of leadership. The use of nonordained leaders to perform ministerial duties was enough of a novelty to draw plenty of criticism, but there were other principles which were equally unique and deserve analysis.

While it may be true that "every great institution is but the lengthened shadow of a great man," Methodism owed as much to its lay leaders as it did to its founder. However, his willingness to share the leadership and to delegate responsibility is as much a credit to him as if he had led the movement singlehandedly. Wesley was no *prima donna*; he was always a team player, and he modeled for his colleagues a collaborative style of directing and decision making. Some of the British social historians like the Webbs, Edward Thompson, Eric Hobsbaum, the Hammonds and others,[25] who are reluctant to recognize Wesley's religious contribution, give him credit nonetheless for creating a pool of working-class leadership from which would later emerge both the Liberal Party and the leadership of the unions. As D. D. Thompson points out:

> Those whom Wesley's appeal reached became changed characters, and the changed character soon expressed itself in changed surroundings; the homes of the Methodists were cleaner than those of their neighbors, their children were cared for and clad, they set about improving their social condition in many ways; they were thrifty, and the training gained in managing their religious societies, and the development of their character which resulted, enabled them to take a leading part in their self-help associations—Friendly Societies, Trade Unions, and Cooperative Societies—which have done so much to elevate and improve the wage-earning classes.[26]

Davies and Rupp in their *History of the Methodist Church in Great Britain*, make somewhat the same observation, but in more sweeping terms:

> The rising social status of Methodism was a tribute to its power as a civilizing influence on converts from the lower orders. Here lay one of its chief contributions to the industrial society now growing up in Britain. In a hundred ways the life of the chapel and class-meeting was an exercise in self-government and an education in social responsibility.... In a rapidly expanding industrial society, strict Methodists were much sought after by employers anxious to find a reliable man for a position of trust. Through increased social mobility, small subordinate posts often led on to great positions. Sir Robert Peel the elder declared in 1787: "I have left most of my works in Lancashire under the management of Methodists and they serve me excellently well."[27]

Two historians who have contributed major scholarly research on the details of Methodist leadership are Maldwyn

Edwards and Robert Wearmouth. Also, individual studies like Robert Moore's *Pittman, Preachers, and Politics: The Effects of Methodism in a Durham Mining Community*[28] provided valuable insights about the work of Methodist lay leaders in particular localities. These and many other recent studies are bolstering the idea that Methodism provided the major training ground for working-class leadership in the eighteenth, nineteenth, and even early twentieth centuries. With this background in mind, it is helpful to examine some of the leadership principles that thrust the working-class Methodists into so many positions of community leadership.

1. *Lay leadership.*

The Methodist movement was largely a revival of lay piety. As an Oxford don, John Wesley had taken his fervent preaching and strenuous discipline to his university colleagues with little success. Even his peers among the established clergy shunned his enthusiastic program. So he took his revival to the people, and he found the leaders for his movement among the uneducated and unordained. Even his leading itinerant preachers refused to arrogate to themselves the title of "Reverend," and they considered themselves only laymen.

Part of the appeal of the Methodist movement was that common laborers had as much opportunity to hold authority-wielding positions as did the professionally trained. In a day when the small man had no place in the government of either church or state, Methodism provided an outlet for their creative energies. In the Methodist chapel, the miner, artisan, and mechanic not only received the ministrations of their peers, but they saw in their leadership patterns a model for whatever aspirations they might have to become leaders.

One author put it this way:

> Methodism provided a field for social leadership. If the layman was still denied a place in the counsels of Conference, he had plenty of scope for responsibility in the many other offices which chapel life had to offer. If

he was adept in financial matters, he could become a steward or trustee. If he had power as a speaker, he became a local preacher. If he excelled as an adviser, he made a good class leader. In itself this was a valuable education. To many of the Durham miners, the building of the chapel was the first lesson in communal effort... the management of the service was an opportunity for the natural leader... the administration of the funds an education in business method. Inside the warm, vibrant life of the chapel they acquired a sense of status in a defined community which was denied them in the world outside, a feeling of self-respect, and of warm fraternity.[29]

2. Appointed leadership, not elected.

Whatever the advantages of democratic leadership selection, Wesley proved the efficiency of appointed leadership. He was strictly opposed to the concept of church leadership by election, and he vowed that no such course would be tolerated during his lifetime. His personal control over the appointments to top positions was, however, tempered by several facts: (1) He sought the counsel of his associates for every appointment, (2) the guidelines for selection were published openly, and (3) he seemed to have a knack for good personnel selection. These three factors seemed to quell most of the opposition to his autocratic rule. Nevertheless, there was a fairly high dropout rate among the itinerant preachers:

It is a remarkable fact that, during Wesley's lifetime, of the 690 men who acted under him as itinerant preachers, 249 relinquished the itinerant ministry. These 249 retirers included not a few of the most intelligent, energetic pious, and useful preachers that Wesley had. Some left him on the ground of health; others began business, because as itinerant preachers they were unable to support their wives and families; but a large proportion became ordained ministers in other churches.[30]

So, Methodism was a training center for both its own societies and for those of other denominations.

Wherever Wesley went to establish a new congregation, he invariably wrote in his *Journal* something like this:

> I appointed several earnest and sensible men to meet me, to whom I showed the great difficulty I had long found of knowing the people who desired to be under my care. After much discourse, they all agreed there could be no better way to come to a sure, thorough knowledge of each person than to divide them into classes like those at Bristol, under the inspection of those in whom I could most confide....[31]

Not only did he retain the right to appoint, but also to recall leaders at every level. Although he allowed considerable differences of opinion on other issues, he never relinquished the tight rein he held over the selection of leaders.

3. *Leaders were recognized and trained, but not made.*

It has often been said that Methodism trained men *in* the ministry, not *for* the ministry. In other words, the early Methodists believed that leadership was a quality which occurred naturally among groups of people and could not be *produced* as such, only recognized and trained. Although training schools for ministers were frequently discussed, there was never any seminary or Bible school for Methodist leaders for well over one hundred years. In fact, there was no formal training program at all during the eighteenth century for them. No academic course "qualified" preachers or would-be-preachers for Methodist appointment. Rather, local people who showed leadership ability were promoted upwards through a succession of minor offices until that ability was recognized at the upper levels by consecration to the itinerancy. Instead of trying to produce leaders, the Methodist system allowed the natural ability of its entire population to rise to its highest potential. In 1746, the Wesleyan preachers established a set of guidelines to evaluate the leadership ability of those who asked for assignment to a preaching post:

> Q. How shall we try those who believe they are moved by the Holy Ghost and called of God to preach?

> A. Inquire:

> 1. Do they know in whom they have believed? Have they the love of God in their hearts? Do they desire and seek nothing but God? And are they holy in all manner of conversation?

> 2. Have they gifts (as well as grace) for the work? Have they (in some tolerable degree) a clear, sound understanding? Have they a right judgment in the things of God? Have they a just conception of the salvation by faith? And has God given them any degree of utterance? Do they speak justly, readily, clearly?

> 3. Have they success? Do they not only speak as generally either to convince or affect the hearts, but have any received remission of sins by their preaching—a clear and lasting sense of the love of God? As long as these three marks undeniably concur in any, we allow him to be called of God to preach. These we receive as sufficient reasonable evidence that he is moved thereto by the Holy Ghost.[32]

The principle of recognizing and training men who are already leaders, rather than trying to make leaders, has been restated in the twentieth century by pioneers in theological education in developing countries. This leadership strategy is one of the major concepts behind the Theological-Education-by-Extension movement which has replaced traditional seminaries in many parts of the developing world. As Covell and Wagner state in their text on extension seminaries:

> Theological educators are now coming to recognize that the task of the seminary is not to *make* leaders. As John Meadowcroft of West Pakistan puts it, "By some kind of metamorphosis, a young fellow who has no qualities of leadership is expected to emerge from the chrysalis of the seminary as a "leader of the community." And he also considers himself to be. The fact, however, is that nothing will make a man a leader if he does not possess the attributes already." The calling of the seminary is to *train* the leaders that God has already made. If this is admitted, the question prior to all others becomes: Whom do we teach?[33]

4. *Qualification by faithfulness.*

A corollary to the practice of recognizing natural leadership is the concept that faithfulness to duty is the primary qualification for positions of authority. Every system of church leadership has its own particular criteria for certification: education, "charisma," speaking ability, popular acclaim, personal magnetism, etc. In the West, education dominates the list. But in developing societies, education is not only an unacceptable test for leadership, it is actually a liability. As Covell and Wagner have pointed out in their studies of church leadership patterns in developing nations:

> They prefer "training in the streets." As a matter of fact, the top leaders consistently turn down lavish scholarship offers, knowing that if they enter some institution

they will lose their status in most of the churches....
Without claiming that there may be a *causal* relationship between the theological level of the pastors and the
evangelical dynamism of their denominations, the existence of correlation between these two facts makes us
less confident of the benefits of theological education,
and even of the method of training in the developed
countries which we impose on Protestants in the developing nations.[34]

In a study by sociologist Christian Lalive D'Epinay, seven
"rungs" of the ladder of ecclesiastical leadership were discovered in
the Pentecostal Methodist Church in Chile, that nation's largest
and fastest-growing denomination:

Anyone can start, in fact all are expected to try the first
rung. Any of the six rungs may break, sending the candidate back to the ranks. The rungs may be described as
follows:

1. *Street preaching*. When a person is converted, he or
she is expected to give his testimony in public in a street
meeting the very next Sunday. Experience will show that
some are gifted and successful in this ministry and if so
they can go up to the next rung.

2. *Sunday school class*. Sunday school meets on Sunday
morning. If the teacher can communicate simple Bible
truths to his students, and hold the interest of his class,
he may be advanced to a more important class, and he
passes this test.

3. "*Preacher.*" As a "preacher" the candidate is permitted
to lead worship and is asked to bring messages on occasion. If his pastor is pleased with his performance, he
will promote him to the following rung.

4. *New preaching point.* When he is sent out to a new preaching point (*avanzada*), his success is measured in an objective way—he must produce converts to demonstrate to others that God has given him the gifts necessary for the ministry. If he does, his position can become official on the next rung.

5. *Christian worker.* Upon application to the Annual Conference of pastors, he is proposed and accepted as a Christian worker (*obrero del Señor*). This gives him an official title for the first time, and he is under the orders of the denominational leadership.

6. *Pastor-deacon.* He is assigned an area (*vina nueva*) in which he is expected to plant a church. As this takes place he may be named pastor-deacon. If he does not gain converts and form the nucleus of a new church, he goes no higher, nor does he receive the title.

7. *Pastor.* The probationer (*probando*) then comes up against his last test. In order to be promoted to pastor, he must present sufficient evidence to the Annual Conference that he can leave the secular world, dedicate his full time to the ministry, and be financially supported in it by the congregation he has gathered together.[35]

This system roughly corresponds to Wesley's "ladder" of leadership: sick-visitor to steward to class-leader to band-leader to local preacher to traveling preacher to assistant in charge of a circuit. The qualification for every level was faithful commitment and service at a lower level. Since education in the eighteenth century was limited to a very few, the priesthood became a social elite, far removed from the world of the common person. But everyone had equal opportunity for faithful service, and therefore for leadership at some level in the Methodist system.

5. *Practice in appealing to action.*

The messages delivered within the Methodist system were exhortations to do something rather than make speeches about something. "Avoid speechifying altogether!" Wesley warned his preachers. Their presentations to the society must call for a decision to act, and that call for action was to be followed with clear explanations on how to do it.

The style of the Methodist preachers might be compared to that of the Greek orator Demosthenes, who was described as follows by one of his contemporaries:

> When his rivals speak, the audience applauds: "What a magnificent speech!" When Demosthenes speaks, the Athenians cry in unison, "Let us march on Philip!"[36]

The Methodists learned in the laboratory of the society meeting the art and skill of drawing a commitment from their audience and getting them to follow through on it. Insipid sermonizing was studiously avoided, and whole generations of local and traveling preachers were schooled in the science of harnessing human motivations. It is no wonder that these men and women trained in the Methodist chapels became the union organizers and community leaders of nineteenth century England.

6. *A combination of local and trans-local leadership.*

John Wesley called his system a "connection," by which he meant an organization of uniform local units held together by a common constitution and a central authority. Each local society was governed by a combination of local and central authority and two types of preachers worked side by side as representatives of their respective jurisdictions. The local preacher was a home-grown member who had emerged from the ranks of the local society; the traveling "assistant" was a member of the central leadership team who was assigned to a certain area or "circuit." In this way a balance was maintained between the wider perspective and the freshness of the itinerant and the cultural identification and local concern of the indigenous preacher. In Wesley's system the itinerant had priority of jurisdiction over the local leadership, although there was a system of checks and balances to keep it from being abused. This cooperation brought together significant elements of vitality and stability and it gave a sense of wider identification to congregations which might otherwise have been isolated.

These six leadership principles, although not unique, combine to form an organizational leadership model which is at once flexible and effective. Its features not only enabled the system to train hundreds of capable leaders at several different levels, but also are universal to be applied in many similar situations at other times in history.

SUPPLEMENTARY INSTRUCTIONAL AIDS

In addition to the group strategies and leadership principles of Methodism, there were other instructional tools which greatly increased the effectiveness of the system. These tools were supplementary to the main functions of the learning groups, but played an important part nonetheless. A few of these tools were: (1) concept formation by hymn singing, (2) penny collections, (3) inexpensive mass publications, (4) primary schools for poor children, and (5) economic development projects for the poor.

1. *Concept formation by hymn singing.*

The Methodists developed a rich and inspiring hymnody which became a hallmark of the movement. At every Methodist meeting (of which, as is now evident, there were many) hymns were sung. Many have given the Methodist hymns high praise as poetical works and as helps to worship. Dr. James Martineau says, "*The Collection of Hymns for the Use of the People Called Methodists,* issued in 1780, was, after the scriptures the grandest instrument of popular religious culture that Christendom has ever produced."[37] Dr. Richard Cadman added his enthusiastic endorsement and evaluation of the Wesleyan hymns:

The most vivid delineation of the inner life of Methodism is found in the hymns of Charles Wesley, which have glorified Christian worship more than any other similar lyrics, with the possible exception of Isaac Watts. They set forth intimate as distinguished from legalistic religion, radiant with the beauty of holiness and the arts of consolation, and overflowing with tenderness....

The realization of divine grace which gave Methodism its first outburst of Christian song had many other far-reaching effects, but none of these compare with the influence of its sacred poetry over all classes, and especially over the poor and illiterate multitudes who were thereby taught to worship God aright.[38]

However, the most significant instructional aspect of Methodist hymnody was that they were written to communicate and inculcate theological concepts. It seems fair to infer that by design the doctrines of Methodism were ingrained in the subconscious minds of its followers by constant repetition, singable tunes, alliterative mnemonic arrangements, and rhyming lines. Not only were the hymns inherently instructive, but the way they were presented tended to enhance the internalization process. The leader "lined out" the hymns by reading one line and waiting for the congregation's choral response, reading the next line, and so on in succession. This pattern of singing is very similar to the question-and-answer format of the catechetical instruction which had been used in the Reformed movements on the continent for nearly two centuries, and with great effect. The cumulative effect of this kind of singing was that the concepts of Methodism became deeply embedded in the minds of the people.

Not only were the Methodists hymn singers, they were also hymn writers. Charles Wesley set the pace for the movement by his composition of over 6,000 hymns, and many others put their religious convictions to verse and tune following his example.

2. Penny collections.

At first glance it might seem unlikely that the mundane practice of taking an offering would have any instructional significance, but apparently it did. It seems that the regular contribution by members reinforced the importance and value of what they were learning and gave the people a sense of ownership about the cause of Methodism. It was *their* class meeting, *their* society, *their* chapel because they had given financial support to it. Their heart was in it. As the biblical aphorism has it, "Where your treasure is, there will your heart be also." And, the contribution of even the poorest kept them from a sense of indebtedness to those who might be perceived as condescending to their level. The penny collections enabled Methodism to be visualized as something that poor people did, rather than as something that was done for them.

3. Inexpensive mass publications.

During his lifetime, John Wesley produced more than four hundred volumes of literature. Some of these were original compositions, some were abridgments, some his own editions of Christian classics, and some collections of writings. The volume and breadth of subject matter (theology, hymnology, medicine, science, education, language, *et al.*) are not the key issues; the wide dissemination of inexpensive and readable materials, especially for the poor, was his main literary contribution. Every Methodist preacher was commissioned to be a bookseller and a promoter of good reading habits.

4. Primary schools for the poor.

Wesley established the first school for miners' children at Kingswood in 1738. This was the beginning of a popular movement to make schooling available to the poor, although it would be over a century before universal and free primary education was available in England. The Kingswood school has been both hailed as a landmark advance for public schooling and maligned as a regressive hindrance, so its place in the history of education is still up for assessment. And, the evaluation of its usefulness is beyond the scope of this book. However, it is significant to Wesley's system that schooling for the children of the poor was an integral branch of the Methodist movement.

5. *Economic development projects for the poor.*

Even though Methodism was a religious movement, the physical necessities of its members demanded immediate economic solutions. On two different fronts Wesley promoted relief and self-help projects. First, he (and other Methodists) designed short-range projects for the unemployed, widows, chronically ill, orphans and physically handicapped. Then, Wesley himself stimulated public philanthropy by appealing for funds for these projects. The combination of Wesley's local projects and George Whitefield's overseas endeavors opened a new era of public charity in Britain, more widespread and less condescending than had been the case in previous generations.

The overall impact of Wesley's system was a massive transformation, even civilization, of the whole bottom level of England's population. Wesley did not conceive a grand design, then leave it to his successors to carry out. He initiated the program of Methodism, guided it through its formative years, then directed its growth through the period of its development as an institution. He lived to see it settled as a permanent system, both in the Old World and in the New, with a competent ministry, well-defined theology, considerable literature, rich hymnody, and the most comprehensive scheme of ecclesiastical discipline outside the Roman Catholic Church.

Wesley seemed to possess that uncanny talent (so essential in great statesmen) of managing at one time the broad outlines and the minute details of a vast system. He could visualize the central government of the "connection" without losing sight of the need of the smallest unit. The system could expand to include thousands of people without dropping its concern for a single individual.

At his death, a commendatory obituary was carried in *The Gentleman's Magazine*, which gives some impression of how he was viewed by the upper classes of his contemporaries:

Whatever may be the opinions held by his inspiration, it is impossible to deny him the merit of having done infinite good to the lower classes of the people. By the humane endeavors of him and his brother Charles a sense of decency in morals and religion was introduced in the lowest classes of mankind, the ignorant were instructed and the wretched relieved and the abandoned reclaimed.... He met with great opposition from many of the clergy and unhandsome treatment from the magistrates.... He was one of the few characters who outlived enmity and prejudices, and received in his later years every mark of esteem from every denomination.... His personal influence was greater perhaps than any private gentleman in the country. All the profit from his literary labors; all that he could receive or collect (and it amounted to an immense sum) was devoted to charitable purposes. Instead of being an ornament to literature, he was a blessing to his fellows; instead of the genius of the age, he was the servant of God.[39]

One of the most poignant analyses of Wesley as an instructional innovator and organizer is this by Abel Stevens:

If Wesley was deficient in what constitutes the highest speculative or philosophic mind, this deficiency itself may have been a necessary qualification for the more utilitarian greatness to which he was appointed. It was necessary that he should be a great legislator in order to render secure his achievements in so many other respects. Speculative philosophers have seldom been good legislators; the history of great men affords not one example of the two characters combined. The Republic of Plato is still an ideal system of beautiful impossibilities to statesmen; the Politics of Aristotle have seldom had a legislative copyist; the Utopia of Sir Thomas More is still a Utopia, the source of proverbial expression to our language, but of no laws to our commonwealths; the new Atlantis of Bacon is yet a dream, notwithstanding its utilitarian suggestions; Locke's Fundamental Constitutions of Carolina were found impracticable; and Rousseau's Contrat Social ranks only as an example of political rhetoric. But John Wesley founded an ecclesiastical system that has only become more efficient by the lapse of a hundred years, and that is acknowledged to be more effective, whether for good or evil, than any other in the Protestant world.[40]

APPENDIX A

Chronology of Major Events Related to the Development of Wesley's Group Models Up to July, 1741

June 17, 1703	Wesley's birth
January 28, 1714	Entered Charterhouse School
June 24, 1720	Entered Oxford University as a student
September 19, 1725	Ordained deacon, Church of England
April—September, 1726	Served as curate at Epworth and Wroote
February 14, 1727	Received M.A. at Oxford
August, 1727	Returned to Epworth and Wroote
November 22, 1729	Returned to Oxford as tutor and joined The Holy Club
October 14, 1735	Sailed for Georgia as chaplain to Oglethorpe
December 22, 1737	Returned to England
February 1, 1738-1739	Attended Moravian groups in London
May 1, 1738	The Fetter Lane Society established
May 24, 1738	The Aldersgate experience
June 15—September 16, 1738	Visit to Herrnhut, Germany
April 1, 1739	The beginning of field preaching
December, 1739	The first Methodist Society at the Foundery
July 20, 1740	The Fetter Lane Society disbanded

APPENDIX B

Orders of a Religious Society
Meeting in Fetter Lane

In obedience to the Command of God by Saint James, and by the Advice of Peter Boehler, May 1, 1738, it was agreed,

1. That they will meet together once in a Week to confess their Faults one to another, and to pray for one another that they may be healed.
2. That any others, of whose sincerity they are well assured, may, if they desire it, meet with them for that Purpose. And, May 29, it was agreed.
3. That the Persons desirous to meet together for that Purpose, be divided into several Bands, or little Societies.
4. That none of these consist of fewer than five, or more than ten Persons.
5. That some Person in each Band be desired to interrogate the rest in order, who may be called the Leader of that Band. And on Monday, September 26, it was agreed,
6. That each Band meet twice in a Week, once on Monday evening, the second time when it is most convenient for each Band.
7. That every Person come punctually at the Hour appointed, without some extraordinary Reason.
8. That those that are present begin exactly at the Hour.
9. That every Meeting be begun and ended with Singing and Prayer.
10. That every one in order speak as freely, plainly, and concisely as he can, the real State of his Heart, with his several Temptations and Deliverances, since the last Time of meeting.
11. That all Bands have a Conference at eight every Wednesday Evening, begun and ended with Singing and Prayer.
12. That Nine of the Clock the Names of the Members be called over, and the Absenters set down.
13. That notice of any extraordinary Meeting be given on the Wednesday night preceding such Meeting.
14. That exactly at ten, if the Business of the Night be not finished, a

short concluding Prayer be used, that those may go who are in haste, but that all depart the Room by half an Hour after ten.

15. That whosoever speaks in this Conference stand up, and that none else speak till he is set down.

16. That nothing which is mentioned in the conference be by any Means mentioned out of it.

17. That every member of this Society, who is a Member of any other, prefer the meeting with this, and with his particular Band, before the meeting with any other Society or Company whatsoever.

18. That if any Person absent himself without some extraordinary Reason, either from his Band, or from any Meeting of the whole Society, he be first privately admonished; and if he be absent again, reprove before the whole Society.

19. That any Person who desires or designs to take any Journey, shall first, if it be possible, have the approbation of the Bands.

20. That all our Members who are in Clubs be desired to withdraw their Names, as being Meetings nowise conducing to the Glory of God.

21. That any who desire to be admitted into this Society be asked, What are your Reasons for desiring this? Will you be entirely open, using no kind of Reserve, least of all in the Case of Love or Courtship? Will you strive against the Desire of ruling, of being first in your Company, or having your own Way? Will you submit to be placed in what Band the Leaders shall choose for you? Have you any objections to any of our Orders? The Orders may then be read to them.

22. That those who answer these Questions in the Affirmative, be proposed every fourth Wednesday.

23. That every one then present speak clearly and fully whatever Objection he has to any Person proposed to be a Member.

24. That those against whom any reasonable Objection appears be acquainted with that Objection, and the admitting them upon Trial postponed till that Objection is removed.

25. That those against whom no reasonable Objection appears or remains, be, in order for their Trial, formed into distinct Bands, and some Person agreed to assist them.

26. That if no new Objection then appear, they be, after two months' Trial, admitted into the Society.

27. That every fourth Saturday be observed as a Day of general Intercession, which may continue from twelve to two, from three to five, and from six to eight.

28. That on Sunday Se'en-night following be a general Love-feast, from seven till ten in the evening.

29. That in order to have a continual Intercession every Member of this

Society choose some Hour, either of the Day or Night, to spend in Prayer chiefly for his Brethren.

30. That in order to a continual Fast, three of the Members of this Society Fast every Day (as their Health permits), Sundays and Holidays excepted, and spend as much as they can of that Day in retirement from Business and

31. That each Person give Notice to the Leader of his Band how much he is willing to subscribe towards the general charge of the Bands, and that each Person's Money be paid in to the Leader of his Band once a month at farthest.

32. That no particular Person be allowed to act in any Thing contrary to any Order of this Society, but that every one, without Distinction, submit to the Determination of his Brethren; and that if any Person or Persons do not, after being thrice admonished, conform to the Society, they be not esteemed any longer as Members.

33. That any person whom the whole Society shall approve may be admitted at our general Meetings, provided he correspond with the Society once in a month at least.

---

*Taken from J. S. Simon, *John Wesley and the Religious Societies*, pp. 196-198.

APPENDIX C

John Wesley's "Preface to the 1739 Hymnbook"*

1. Some Verses it may be observed, in the following Collection, were wrote upon the scheme of the Mystic divines. And these, 'tis owned, we had once in great veneration, as the best explainers of the Gospel of Christ. But we are now convinced that we therein greatly erred: not knowing the Scriptures, neither the power of God. And because this is an error which many serious minds are sooner or later exposed to, and which indeed most easily besets those who seek the Lord Jesus in sincerity, we believe ourselves indispensably obliged in the presence of God, and angels, and men, to declare wherein we apprehend those writers not to teach the truth as it is in Jesus.

2. And first, we apprehend them to lay another foundation. They are careful indeed to pull down our own works, and to prove, that be-the Deeds of the law shall no flesh be justified. But why is this? Only, to establish our own righteousness in the place of our own works. They speak largely and well against expecting to be accepted of God for our virtuous actions; and then teach, that we are to be accepted for our virtuous habits or tempers. Still the ground of our acceptance is placed in ourselves. The difference is only this: Common writers suppose we are to be justified for the sake of our outward righteousness. These suppose we are to be justified for the sake of our inward righteousness: whereas, in truth, we are no more justified for the sake of one than of the other. For neither our own inward nor outward righteousness is the ground of our justification. Holiness of heart, as well as holiness of life, is not the cause, but the effect of it. The sole cause of our acceptance with God (or, that for the sake of which, on the account of which, we are accepted) is the righteousness and the death of Christ, who fulfilled God's law, and died in our stead. And even the condition of it is not (as they suppose) our holiness either or heart or life: but our faith alone; faith contradistinguished from holiness as well as from good works. Other foundation therefore can no man lay, without being an adversary to Christ and His Gospel, than faith alone, faith though necessarily producing both, yet not including either good works or holiness.

3. But supposing them to have laid the foundation right, the manner of building thereon which they advise is quite opposite to that prescribed by Christ. He commands to build up one another. They advise, "To the desert, to the desert, and God will build you up." Numberless are the commendations that occur in all their writings, not of retirement inter-mixed with conversation, but of an entire seclusion from men, (perhaps for months or years), in order to purify the soul. Whereas, according to the judgment of our Lord, and the writings of His apostles, it is only when we are knit together, that we have nourishment from Him, and increase with the increase of God. Neither is there any time when the weakest member can say to the strongest, or the strongest to the weakest, "I have no need of thee." Accordingly our blessed Lord, when His disciples were in their weakest state, sent them forth, not alone, but two by two. When they were strengthened a little, not by solitude, but by abiding with Him and one another, He commanded them to wait, not separate, but being assembled together, for the promise of the Father. And they were all with one accord in one place, when they received the gift of the Holy Ghost. express mention is made three thousand souls, all that believed were together, and continued steadfastly not only in the apostles' doctrine, but also in fellowship, and in breaking of bread, and in praying with one accord. Agreeable to which is the account the great apostle gives of the manner which he had been taught of God, for the perfecting of the saints, for the edifying of the body of Christ, even to the end of the world. And, according to Saint Paul, all who will ever come, in the unity of the faith, unto a perfect man, unto the measure of the stature of the fullness of Christ, must together grow up into Him: from whom the whole body fitly joined together and compacted (or strengthened) by that which every joint supplieth, according to the effectual working in the measure of every part, maketh increase of the Body unto the edifying of itself in love. (Ephesians iv:15,16)

4. So widely distant is the manner of building up souls in Christ taught by Saint Paul, from that taught by the Mystics! Nor do they differ as to the foundation, or the manner of building thereon, more than they do with regard to the structure. For the religion these authors would edify us in is solitary religion. If thou wilt be perfect, say they, "trouble not thyself about outward works. It is better to work virtues in the will. He hath attained the true resignation, who hath estranged himself from all outward works, that God may work inwardly in him, without any turning to outward things. These are the true worshipers, who worship God in spirit and in truth." For contemplation is with them the fulfilling of the law, even a contemplation that "consists in a cessation of all works."

5. Directly opposite to this is the Gospel of Christ. Solitary religion is not to be found there. "Holy solitaries" is a phrase no more consistent with the Gospel than holy adulterers. The Gospel of Chirst knows of no religion, but social; no holiness, but social holiness. Faith working by love is the length and breadth and depth and height of Christian perfection. This commandment have we from Christ, that he who loves God, love his brother also; and that we manifest our love by doing good unto all men, especially to them that are of the household of faith. And, in truth, whosoever loveth his brethren not in word only, but as Christ loved him, cannot but be zealous of good works. He feels in his soul a burning, restless desire of spending and being spent for them. My Father, will he say, worketh hitherto, and I work: and, at all possible opportunities, he is, like his Master, going about doing good.

6. This then is the way: walk ye in it, whosoever ye are that have believed in His name. Ye know, other foundation can no man lay, than that which is laid, even in Jesus Christ. Ye feel that by grace ye are saved through faith; saved from sin, by Christ formed in your hearts, and from fear, by His Spirit bearing witness with your spirit, that ye are the sons of God. Ye are taught of God, not to forsake the assembling of yourselves together, as the manner of some is; but to instruct, admonish, exhort, reprove, comfort, confirm, and every way build up one another. Ye have an unction from the Holy One, that teacheth you to renounce any other or higher perfection, than faith working by love, faith zealous of good works, faith as it hath opportunity doing good unto all men. As ye have therefore received Jesus Christ the Lord, so walk ye in Him: rooted and built up in Him, and stablished in the faith, and abounding therein more and more. Only, beware lest any man spoil you through philosophy and vain deceit, after the tradition of men, after the rudiments of the world, and not after Christ. For ye are complete in Him. He is Alpha and Omega, the beginning and the endings, the first and the last. Only continue in Him, grounded and settled, and be not moved away from the hope of the Gospel; and when Christ, who is our life, shall appear, then shall ye also appear with Him in glory!

---

*From *The Poetical Works of John and Charles Wesley*, collected and arranged by G. Osborn (London: Wesleyan Methodist Conference Office, 1868), I:ix-xxiii.

APPENDIX D

Twelve Rules of a Helper*

1. Be diligent. Never be unemployed a moment: never be triflingly employed. Never while away time; neither spend any more time at any place than is strictly necessary.

2. Be serious. Let your motto be, Holiness to the Lord. Avoid all lightness, jesting, and foolish talking.

3. Converse sparingly and cautiously with women: particularly with young women in private.

4. Take no step towards marriage without first acquainting us with your design.

5. Believe evil of no one; unless you see it done, take heed how you credit it. Put the best construction on everything: you know the judge is always supposed to be on the prisoner's side.

6. Speak evil of no one; else your word, especially, would eat as doth a canker. Keep your thoughts within your own breast, till you come to the person concerned.

7. Tell every one what you think wrong in him, and that plainly, and as soon as may be, else it will fester in your heart. Make all haste to cast the fire out of your bosom.

8. Do not affect the gentleman. You have no more to do with this character than with that of a dancing-master. A preacher of the gospel is the servant of all.

9. Be ashamed of nothing but sin; not of fetching wood (if time permit) or of drawing water; not of cleaning your own shoes, or your neighbour's.

10. Be punctual. Do everything exactly at the time: and, in general, do not mend our rules, but keep them; not for wrath, but for conscience sake.

11. You have nothing to do but to save souls. Therefore spend and be spent in this work. And so always, not only to those who want you, but to those who want you most.

12. Act in all things, not according to your own will, but as a son in the gospel. As such, it is your part to employ your time in the manner which we direct; partly in preaching and visiting the flock from house to house; partly in reading, meditation, and prayer. Above all, if you labour with us in our Lord's vineyard, it is needful that you should do that part of the work which we advise, at those times and places which we judge most for his glory.

---

*From Southey, Life of Wesley, pp. 72-73.

BIBLIOGRAPHY

Andrews, Stuart. *Methodism and Society*. London: Longman Group Ltd., 1970.

Armstrong, Anthony. *The Church of England, the Methodists, and Society*. Totowa, New Jersey: Rowman and Littlefield, 1973.

Atkinson, John. *The Class Leader: His Work and How to Do It*. New York: Phillips and Hunt, 1874.

Baker, Eric W. *A Herald of the Evangelical Revival: A Critical Inquiry into the Relation of William Law to John Wesley and the Beginnings of Methodism*. London: The Epworth Press, 1948.

Barr, Josiah Henry. *Early Methodists Under Persecution*. New York: The Methodist Book Concern, 1916.

Bashford, James W. *Wesley and Goethe*. Cincinnati: Jennings and Pye, 1903.

Bennett, Richard. *The Early Life of Howell Harris*. London: Banner of Truth Trust, 1962.

Bett, Henry. "A French Marquis and the Class Meeting." *Proceedings of the Wesleyan Historical Society*, XVIII:43-56, September, l931.

Cadman, S. Parkes. *The Three Religious Leaders of Oxford and Their Movements: John Wycliffe, John Wesley, and John Henry Newman*. New York: The Macmillan Company, 1916.

Cameron, Richard. *The Rise of Methodism*. New York: The Philosophical Library, 1954.

Carter, Henry. *The Methodist: A Study in Discipleship*. London: Charles H. Kelly, 1914.

_____. *The Methodist Heritage*. London: Epworth Press, 1951

Carvosso, William. *A Memoir of Mr. William Carvosso, Sixty Years a Class Leader in the Wesleyan Methodist Connection*, New York: Carlton and Lanaham, 1835.

Cell, George Croft. *The Rediscovery of John Wesley*. New York: Henry Holt and Company, 1935.

Christophers, S. W. *Class-meetings in Relation to the Design and Success of Methodism*. London: Wesleyan Conference Office, 1873.

Church, Leslie F. *More About the Early Methodist People*. London: The Epworth Press, 1949.

_____. *The Early Methodist People*. New York: Philosophical Library, 1949.

Covell, Ralph R. and C. Peter Wagner. *An Extension Seminary Primer*. South Pasadena, California: William Carey Library, 1971.

Dallimore, Arnold A. *George Whitefield: The Life and Times of the Great Evangelist of the Eighteenth Century Revival*, Volume I. London: Banner of Truth Trust, 1970.

Davies, Rupert and Gordon Rupp, eds. *A History of the Methodist Church in Great Britain*. London Epworth Press, 1965.

Dimond, Sydney G. *The Psycholoqy of Methodism*. London: Epworth Press, 1932.

Dolbey, George W. *The Architectural Expressions of Methodism*. London: Epworth Press, 1964.

Drakeford, John Wesley. *People to People Therapy* New York: Harper and Row, 1978.

Edwards, Maldwyn. *After Wesley*. London: Epworth Press, 1938.

_____. *Methodism and England, A Study of Methodism in its Social and Political Aspects During the Period 1850-1932*. London: Epworth Press, 1943.

Emerick, Samuel. *Spiritual Renewal for Methodism*. Nashville: The Methodist Evangelistic Materials, l958.

Emory, John, ed. *The Works of the Reverend John Wesley, A.M.* New York: Waugh and Mason, 1835.

Emory, Robert. *The History of the Discipline of the Methodist Episcopal Church*. New York: Carlton and Porter, 1857.

Ethridge, Willie Snow. *Strange Fires: The True Story of John Wesley's Love Affair in Georgia*. New York: The Vanguard Press, Inc., 1971.

Fitzgerald, O. P. *The Class Meeting.* Nashville: M. E. Church, South, Publishing House, 1880.

Fitzgerald, W. B. *The Roots of Methodism.* London: Charles H. Kelly, 1903.

Gillies, John, ed. *Memoirs of the Reverend George Whitefield.* New Haven: Whitmore and Buckingham and H. Mansfield, 1834.

Goodell, Charles L. *The Drillmaster of Methodism: Principles and Methods for the Class Leader and Pastor.* New York: Eaton and Mains, 1902.

_____. Green, J. Brazier. *John Wesley and William Law.* London: Epworth Press, 1945.

Green, Richard. *The Conversion of John Wesley.* London: Epworth Press, 1908.

Green, V. H. H. *John Wesley.* New York: Saint Martins Press, 1961.

Gregory, Benjamin. *A Handbook of Wesleyan Methodist Polity and History.* London: Wesleyan Methodist Bookroom, 1888.

Halevy, Elie. *The Birth of Methodism in England.* Tr. Bernard Semmel. Chicago: University of Chicago Press, 1971.

Hammond, J. L. and Barbara Hammond. *The Age of the Chartists, 1832-1854: A Study of Discontent.* London: Longmans, Green, and Co., 1930.

Henkle, Moses M. *Primary Platform of Methodism, or Exposition of the General Rules.* Louisville: Southern Methodist Book Concern, 1851.

Henry, Stuart C. *George Whitefield: Wayfaring Witness.* New York: Abingdon Press, 1957.

Hobhouse, Stephen, ed. *Selected Mystical Writings of William Law.* New York: Harper and Brothers Publishers, 1948.

Hobley, L. F. *Working-class and Democratic Movements.* Glasgow: Blackie and Son, Ltd., 1970.

Hoffer, Eric. *The True Believer.* New York: Harper and Row, 1951.

Jackson, Thomas, ed. *The Works of the Reverend John Wesley A. M.* London: John Mason, 1830.

James, William. *The Varieties of Religious Experience.* New York: The Modern Library, 1936.

Jessop, William. *An Account of Methodism in Rossendale and the Neighborhood.* Manchester: Tubbs, Brook and Chrystal, 1880.

Kallstad, Thorvald. *John Wesley and the Bible: A Psychological Study.* Stockholm: Nya Bokforlags Aktiebolaget, 1974.

Kettlewell, S. *Thomas a Kempis and the Brothers of the Common Life.* London: Kegan Paul, Trench and Co., 1885.

Know, Ronald. *Enthusiasm: A Chapter in the History of Religion, with Special References to the XVII and XVIII Centuries.* Oxford: Clarendon Press, 1950.

Law, William. *A Serious Call to a Devout and Holy Life, Adapted to the State and Condition of all Orders of Christians.* London: William Phillipps, 1815.

Lecky, William Edward Hartpole. *A History of England in the Eighteenth Century.* London: Longman's Green and Co., 1883.

Luccock, Halford E., Paul Hutchinson, and Robert Goodloe. *The Story of Methodism.* New York: Abingdon Press, 1949.

McLeish, John. *Evangelical Religion and Popular Education.* London: Methuen and Co. Ltd., 1969.

McLuhan, Marshall. *The Gutenberg Galaxy: The Making of Typographic Man.* Toronto: University of Toronto Press, 1962.

_____. *Understanding Media: The Extensions of Man.* New York: McGraw Hill, 1964.

McTyeire, Holland N. *A History of Methodism.* Nashville: Publishing House of the M. E. Church, South, 1904.

Mailer, Norman. *Armies of the Night.* New York: The New American Library, 1968.

Matthews, H. F. *Methodism and the Education of the People, 1791-1851.* London: The Epworth Press, 1949.

Miley, John. *A Treatise on Class Meetings.* Cincinnati: Swormstedt and Poe, 1854.

Moore, Robert. *Pitmen, Preachers and Politics: The Effects of Methodism in a Durham Mining Community.* Cambridge: University Press, 1974.

Newton, John A. *Susanna Wesley and the Puritan Tradition in Methodism.* London: Epworth Press, 1968.

North, Eric McCoy. *Early Methodist Philanthropy.* New York: The Methodist Book Concern, 1914.

Nuttall, Geoffrey Fillingham. *Howell Harris, 1714-1773: The Last Enthusiast.* Cardiff: University of Wales, 1955.

Outler, Albert C., ed. *John Wesley.* Oxford: Oxford University Press, 1964.

Parkinson, F. M. "Class Tickets" *Proceedings of the Wesleyan Historical Society*, Vol. 1, Part 5, pp. 129-136.

Piette, Maximin.*John Wesley in the Evolution of Protestantism.* London: Sheed and Ward, 1938.

Pollock, John. *George Whitefield and the Great Awakening.* Garden City: Doubleday and Company, 1972.

Prince, John W. *Wesley Religious Education.* New York: The Methodist Book Concern, 1926.

Rattenbury, J. Ernest. *The Conversion of the Wesleys: A Critical Study.* London: The Epworth Press, 1938.

Rigg, James H. *The Connexional Economy of Wesleyan Methodism in its Ecclesiastical and Spiritual Aspects.* London: Wesley Conference Office, 1879.

Robb, Mary Cooper, ed. *The Life of Christian Devotion: Devotional Selections from the Works of William Law.* Nashville: Abingdon Press, 1961.

Roberts, Griffith T. *Howell Harris.* London: Epworth Press, 1951.

Rosser, L. *Class Meetings: Embracing Their Origin, Nature Obligations, and Benefits.* Richmond, Virginia: L. Johnson Co., 1855.

Sangster, Paul. *Pity My Simplicity: The Evangelical Revival and the Religious Education of Children, 1738-1800.* London: Epworth Press, 1963.

Schmidt, Martin. *John Wesley: A Theological Biography.* Tr. Norman P. Goldhawk. London Epworth Press, 1962.

Semmel, Bernard. *The Methodist Revolution.* New York: Basic Books, 1974.

Simon, John S. *John Wesley and the Methodist Societies.* London: Epworth Press, 1952.

_____. *John Wesley and the Religious Societies.* London: Epworth Press, 1921.

Smith, Alan. *The Established Church and Organized Religion, 1750-1850.* London: Longman Group Ltd., 1970.

Southey, Robert. *The Life of Wesley, and the Rise and Progress of Methodism.* Oxford: Oxford University Press, 1925.

Spangenberg, A. G. *The Life of Nicholas Louis Count Zlnzendorf.* Tr. by B. LaTrobe. London: publisher unknown, 1828.

Sproull, Jerry. *The Class Meeting.* Th.M. thesis, Asbury Theological Seminary, Wilmore, KY, 1967.

Stevens Abel. *Character Sketches.* New York: Eaton and Mains, 1888.

Stevenson, George J. *City Road Chapel, London, and its Associations.* London: (author), 1872.

Telford, John. *The Letters of the Reverend John Wesley A. M.* London: Epworth Press, 1957.

_____. *The Life of Wesley.* New York: Eaton and Mains, n.d.

_____. *The Methodist Hymn-book Illustrated.* Second edition. London: Robert Culley, 1909.

Thompson, D. D. *John Wesley as a Social Reformer.* New York: Eaton and Mains, 1898.

Towlson, Clifford W. *Moravian and Methodist: Relationships and Influences in the Eighteenth Century.* London: Epworth Press, 1957.

Tuttle, Robert G., Jr. *John Wesley: His Life and Theology.* Grand Rapids: Zondervan, 1958.

Tyerman, Luke. *The Life of the Reverend George Whitefield.* Two volumes. London: Hodder and Stoughton, 1876.

_____. *The Life and Times of the Reverend John Wesley, M. A.* New York: Harper and Brothers, 1872.

Ward, J. T. *Chartism*. London: B. T. Batsford Ltd., 1973.

Warner, Wellman J. *The Wesleyan Movement in the Industrial Revolution*. London: Lonamans, Green, and Co., 1930.

Wearmouth, Robert E. *Methodism and the Common People of the Eighteenth Century*. London: Epworth Press, 1945.

_____. *Methodism and the Struggle of the Working Classes, 1800-1850*. Leicester, England: Edgar Backus, 1954.

Weber, Max. *The Protestant Ethic and the Spirit of Capitalism*. Tr. by Talcott Parsons; New York: Charles Scribner's Sons, 1958.

Wedgewood, Julia. *John Wesley and the Evangelical Reaction of the Eighteenth Century*. London: Macmillan and Co., 1870

Wesley, John. *An Extract from Mr. Law's Serious Call to A Holy Life*. New York: Carlton and Phillips, 1853.

Whitefield, George. *Journals*. London: Banner of Truth Trust, 1960.

Whitehead, Alfred North. *The Aims of Education and Other Essays*. New York: The Macmillan Company, 1929.

Wright, J. D. "Class and Band Tickets." *Proceedings of the Wesleyan Historical Society*, Vol. V, Part 2, pp. 33-44.

Notes

Introduction

1. "Letter to Vincent Perronet," Works, VIII.

2. Matthew 28:20

CHAPTER ONE—THE WESLEYAN REVOLUTION

1. H. F. Matthews, *Methodism and the Education of the People*, (London: The Epworth Press), p. 11.

2. V. H. H. Green, *John Wesley* (New York: St. Martin's Press, 1961) p. 12.

3. Alan Smith, *The Established Church and Organized Religion, 1750-1850* (London: Longman Group Ltd., 1970) provides a good overview of the religious situation.

4. An interesting study of the term in Ronald Knox's Enthusiasm: *A Chapter in the History of Religion, with Special Reference to the XVII and XVIII Centuries* (Oxford: Clarendon Press, 1950). Knox's book contains a segment on Wesley as an "enthusiast." Symptomatic of the fears associated with "enthusiasm" is the Bampton Lecture Series for 1802, given at Oxford by George Frederick Nott and published Oxford University Press under the title *Religious Enthusiasm Considered*.

5. *Works*, IX:446-509, quoted in Maximums Piette, *John Wesley in the Evolution of Protestantism* (London: Sheed and Ward, 1938), p. 416.

6. Arnold A. Dallimore, *George Whitefield: The Life and Times of the Great Evangelist of the Eighteenth Century Revival* (London: Banner of Truth Trust, 1970), Vol. I., pp. 103-117, "Preaching That Startled a Nation."

7. *Memoirs of the Life and Writing of Benjamin Franklin*, I:87.

8. Pollock, *George Whitefield and the Great Awakening*, p. 121.

9. Some good biographies of *Howell Harris* are: Griffith T. Roberts, Howell Harris (London: The Epworth Press, 1951); Richard Bennett, *The Early Life of Howell Harris* (London: Banner of Truth Trust, 1962); and Geoffrey Fillingham Nuttall, *Howell Harris, 1714-1773: The Last Enthusiast* (Cardiff: University of Wales Press, 1955).

10. Roberts, *Howell Harris*, p. 110.

11. Pollock, *George Whitefield, p. 81.*

12. Latimer's *Annals of Bristol in the Eighteenth Century*, pp. 107-202, quoted in Simon, *John Wesley and the Religious Societies*, pp. 259-260.

13. Pollock, *George Whitefield*, p. 40.

14. Whitefield's *Journals*, p. 216. His text was Matthew 5:1-3.

15. Ibid.

16. John Gillies, ed., *Memoirs of the Reverend George Whitefield*, (New Haven: Whitmore and Buckingham and H. Mansfield, 1834), p. 28.

17. Dallimore, p. 272.

18. Simon, pp. 223-224.

19. *Journal*, II:167.

20. *Journal*, II;209.

21. Quoted in Martin Schmidt, *John Wesley: A Theological Biography*, 2 volumes, tr. Norman P. Goldhawk (London: The Epworth Press, 1962) II:72-73.

22. In the nineteenth century, one popular way of interpreting the eighteenth century historically was to contrast the English and French responses to the industrial revolution. Frequently, Wesley and Voltaire were pitted opposite each other as the archetypes of their respective national personalities. The idea that Wesley's movement enabled England to avoid a violent revolution was a popular theme given scholarly status by the French historian Elie Halevy (*The Birth of the Methodism in England*, tr. Bernard Semmel, Chicago: The University of Chicago Press, 1971). Subsequent interpreters of English history have generally ranged themselves on one side or the other of Halevy's thesis. For a helpful historiographical overview and critique of this question, see the preface to Robert Moore's *Pitmen, Preachers, and Politics: The Effects of Methodism in a Durham Mining Community*, Cambridge University Press, 1974.

23. Holland M. McTyeire, *History of Methodism* (Nashville: Publishing House of the M. E. Church, South, 1904), p. 204.

CHAPTER TWO—THE FORMATION OF WESLEY'S METHOD

1. Schmidt, *John Wesley*, trans. Norman P. Goldhawk.

2. Luke Tyerman, *The Life and Times of the Reverend Samuel Wesley, M.A.* (New York: Harper and Brothers, 1872), p. 125.

3. John A. Newton, *Susanna Wesley and the Puritan Tradition in Methodism* (London: Epworth Press, 1968), p. 114.

4. Ibid., p. 78.

5. A popular Wesleyan story, although without historical verification, is that John Wesley discovered a manuscript in the garret of the old rectory, written by his father. It is said to have contained a scheme for world evangelization which John then put to use. For example, see Newell Dwight Hillis, *Great Men as Prophets of a New Era* (New York: Fleming H. Revell Co., 1922), p. 153.

6. Newton, *Susanna Wesley*, pp. 87-88. Also, Clarke, *Wesley Family*, I:198-199.

7. For a good bibliographic summary on Susanna Wesley see the introduction to Newton's *Susanna Wesley*.

8. Unfortunately, this explanation of her views on the Anglican/Puritan controversy was lost in the fire which swept the Wesley parsonage.

9. Scupoli's *Pugna Spiritualis (Spiritual Conflict)* was apparently a favorite devotional book of Susanna's. Written by a Italian monk of the Theatine Order, this book had become known in England through a Spanish translation by Juan de Castaniza. Cf. Newton, *Susanna Wesley*, p. 136.

10. Ibid.

11. *Journal* (July 24, 1732), III:34.

12. Issac Taylor, *Wesley and Methodism* (New York: Harper and Brothers, 1852), p. 217.

13. Henri Talon, in his excellent biography of John Bunyan, gives a fine study of the Puritan home. On page 191, he says, "We must see the

Puritan home if we really want to understand him; only then a whole leg-end collapses." Dr. Annesley's interest in family life is illustrated by the books in his library on the subject: not only did he have the *Poor Man's Family Book, The Christian Directory*, and the *Reformed Pastor* by Baxter, but also *A Parents' Primmer*, Stockton's *Family Instruction*, Williams's *Vanity of Childhood*, and Lamb's *Religious Family*. Cf. Newton, *Susanna Wesley*, p. 52.

14. Newton, *Susanna Wesley*, p. 53.

15. Ibid., p. 77.

16. McTyeire, *A History of Methodism*, pp. 44-45.

17. Anthony Armstrong, *The Church of England, The Methodists, and Society* (Totowa, New Jersey: Rowman and Littlefield, 1973), p. 56.

18. This letter is quoted in Newton, *Susanna Wesley*, p. 55.

19. Schmidt, *John Wesley*, I:63.

20. "John entered the Charterhouse School, London, at eleven years of age, on the nomination of the Duke of Buckingham, and remained there until he was seventeen. It consisted of a brotherhood for eighty poor men and a school for forty poor boys. The latter has ranked as one of the fore-most public schools of the realm, and boasts among its scholars the names of Crashaw, Lovelace, Barrow, Roger Williams, Addison, Steele, Wesley, Blackstone, Grote, Thirlwall, Leech, Havelock, and Thackeray." S. Parkes Cadman, *Three Religious Leaders of Oxford and Their Movements: John Wycliffe, John Wesley, and John Henry Newman* (New York: The McMillan Company, 1916), p. 188.

21. John Telford, *The Life of John Wesley*, p. 33.

22. *Works*, XI:366-367, also Cadman, *Three Religious Leaders*, p. 193-194, and Albert C. Outler ed., *John Wesley* (New York: Oxford University Press, 1964), pp. 6-8.

23. Clarke, *Wesley Family*, I:293; Tyerman, *Life and Times of the Reverend Samuel Wesley*, pp 391-392; and Newton, *Susanna Wesley*, p. 86.

24. John Wesley, Works, XI: 366-367; *Journal*, I:449-484 (May 24, 1738); "A Plain Account of Christian Perfection: Part II," *Works*, XI:367; also the sermon "On Numbers 23:23," Works, VII:419-30.

25. *Letters*, I:34.

26. Schmidt, *John Wesley*, I:96-97.

27. Tyerman, *Life and Times of John Wesley*, I:69-70.

28. A complete description of the activities of the Holy Club is given in a letter by one of its original members, John Gambold, published in McTyeire's *History of Methodism*, pp. 58-59.

29. For an analysis of the influence of the Religious Societies on both Methodism and the Church of England, see Tyerman, *Life and Times of John Wesley*, I:254; Schmidt, *John Wesley*, I:33; and Albert Outler, ed., *John Wesley* (Oxford: University Press, 1964), p. 307.

30. John Walsh, *Essays in Modern English Church History*, ed., C. V. Bennett (New York: Oxford University Press, 1966), p. 144.

31. Nutall, *Howell Harris, 1714-1773: The Last Enthusiast.*

32. Walsh, *Essays in Modern English Church History*, p. 145 and Tyerman, *Life and Times of John Wesley*, I:87.

33. Ibid., I:73.

34. Cadman, *The Three Religious Leaders of Oxford*, p. 202.

35. Ibid., p. 207.

36. *Journal*, I:197-205.

37. For a thorough evaluation of the relationship between Wesley's groups and the Religious Societies, see J. S. Simon, *John Wesley and the Religious Societies* (London: The Epworth Press, 1921).

38. Schmidt, *John Wesley*, I:134.

39. Works, XII:35. See also Tyerman, *Life and Times of John Wesley*, I:116 and Cadman, *Three Religious Leaders of Oxford*, p. 206.

40. Two interesting analyses which seem to bear out this conclusion are Wellman J. Warner, *The Wesleyan Movement in the Industrial Revolution* (London: Longmans, Green, and Co., 1930) and Robert E. Wearmouth, *Methodism and the Common People of the Eighteenth Century* (London: The Epworth Press, 1945).

41. John Wesley, ed., *An extract of the life of Monsieur de Renty, a Late Nobleman of France*, abridged from a biography by Jean Baptiste de St. Jude, third edition (Briston: 1760), p. 5.

42. Ibid., p. 6.

43. Henry Bett, "A French Marquis and the Class Meeting," *Proceedings of the Wesley Historical Society*, XVIII:43-46, September, 1931.

44. *Journal*, I:71-72.

45. Wesley, *Life of de Renty*, p. 6.

46. Ibid., p. 14.

47. Bett, "A French Marquis and the Class Meeting," p. 45.

48. Ibid., p. 44.

49. *Works*, VIII:46.

50. Wesley's extract was from *The Holy Life of Monr. de Renty, a Late Nobleman of France and Sometimes Counsellor to King Lewis the 13th* which was written in French by John Baptist St. Jude and translated into English by E. S. Gent. It was published in London by John Crook "at the Sign of the Ship in St. Paul's Churchyard" in 1658.

51. Wesley, *Life of de Renty*, preface.

52. Ibid., p. 47.

53. For additional comparison of Wesley's groups to those of de Renty, see Schmidt, *John Wesley* I:191-192.

54. Outler, *John Wesley*, p. 353.

55. Piette, *John Wesley in the Evolution of Protestantism*, p. 186.

56. Clifford W. Towlson, *Moravian and Methodist* (London: The Epworth Press, 1957), pp. 17-18.

57. Ibid.

58. Ibid.

59. General Oglethorpe was the largest subscriber to Samuel Wesley's *Commentary on Job* (Samuel was John Wesley's father). Cadman, *Three Religious Leaders* of Oxford, p. 207.

60. He translated 36 Moravian hymns altogether and makes this comment regarding their origin: "I translated many of their hymns, for the use of our own congregations. Indeed, as I durst not implicitly follow any man, I did not take all that lay before me, but selected those which I judged to be most scriptural, and most suitable to sound experience." This quote from his sermon "On Knowing Christ After the Flesh" is discussed in Towlson, *Moravian and Methodist*, pp. 201-202.

61. *Journal*, I:141-143, Sunday, January 25, 1736.

62. Ibid.

63. J. Ernest Rattenbury, *The Conversion of the Wesleys: A Critical Study* (London: The Epworth Press, 1938), 62.

64. Richard Green, *The Conversion of John Wesley* (London: The Epworth Press, 1937), pp. 29-30.

65. For a complete analysis of Wesley's love affair with Miss Hopkey see Willie Snow Ethridge, *Strange Fires: The True Story of John Wesley's Love Affair in Georgia* (New York: The Vanguard Press, Inc., 1971).

66. Cadman, *Three Religious Leaders of Oxford*, p. 223.

67. Wesley recorded in his *Journal* for Saturday, April 22, 1738, "I could not understand how this faith should be given in a moment: how a man could at once be thus turned from darkness to light, from sin and misery to rightousness and joy in the Holy Ghost. I searched the Scriptures again touching this very thing, particularly the Acts of the Apostles, but to my utter astonishment, found scarce any instances there of other than instantaneous conversions; scarce any so slow as that of St. Paul, who was three days in the pangs of new birth. I had but one retreat left; namely, 'Thus, I grant, God wrought in the first ages of Christianity; but the times are changed. What reasons have I to believe He works in the same manner now?' But on Sunday the 23rd I was brought out of this retreat too, by the concurring evidence of several living witnesses; who testified God had thus wrought in themselves, giving them in a moment such a faith in the blood of His Son as translated them out of darkness into light, out of sin and fear into holiness and happiness. Here ended my disputing. I could now only cry out 'Lord, help Thou my unbelief!'"

68. Quoted in Richard Green, *The Conversion of John Wesley*, p. 33.

69. *Journal*, Wednesday, May 24, 1738.

70. One interesting detractor from the significance of John Wesley's Aldersgate experience, who sees it as a nineteenth-century misinterpretation of the event is Maximin Piette's contained in his thesis *John Wesley in the Evolution of Protestantism*. See especially p. 305 ff.

71. William Edward Hartpole Lecky, *A History of England in the Eighteenth Century* (London: Longmans, Green and Co., 1883), II:558.

72. Quoted in Rattenbury, *The Conversion of the Wesleys*, p. 24.

73. George Croft Cell, *The Rediscovery of John Wesley* (New York: Henry Holt and Company, 1935), p. 185.

74. *Works*, VIII:468.

75. Julia Wedgwood, *John Wesley and the Evangelical Reaction of the Eighteenth Century* (New York: Henry Holt and Company, 1935), p. 185.

76. Cadman, *Three Religious Leaders of Oxford*, p. 288.

77. A. G. Spangenberg, *The Life of Nicholas Louis Count Zinzendorf*, trans. B. LaTrobe, 1838, pp. 86-87. See also, Towlson, *Moravian and Methodist*, p. 185.

78. *Journal*, August, 1738, II:50.

79. Ibid., II:53.

80. *Journal*, II:496.

81. Towlson, *Moravian and Methodist*, p. 38.

82. *Journal*, Curnock's footnote, II:25.

83. Towlson, *Moravian and Methodist*, p. 18.

84. Letter to Church at Herrnhut, October 15, 1738; *Journal*, fn. II:92.

85. Letter to Charles Wesley, April 21, 1741; *Journal* II:448-449.

86. Outler, *John Wesley*, p. 353.

87. *Journal*, I:198, for May 1, 1738.

88. Ibid.

89. Towlson, *Moravian and Methodist*, p. 188.

90. Ibid. Towlson includes in his analysis of the Fetter Lane Society a list of those practices which he feels were Wesley's original contributions.

91. Simon, *John Wesley and the Religious Societies*, p. 296.

92. For a study on the relationship between the Moravian idea of priesthood of believers and the Wesleyan use of lay preachers see Towlson, *Moravian and Methodist*, chapter 5, pp. 105-137.

93. Dallimore, *George Whitefield*, Vol. I., pp. 174-175.

94. *Journal*, I:198, footnote.

95. Simon, *John Wesley and the Religious Societies*, pp. 296-297.

96. Henry, *George Whitefield*, pp. 14-19.

97. Dallimore, pp. 143-162.

98. Ibid., p. 203.

99. *Works* IV:1-6.

100. *Works*, VIII:37-38, Letters, II:296-297.

101. Simon, *John Wesley and the Religious Societies*, p. 327.

102. Ibid., p. 324. Emphasis mine.

103. *Works*, VIII:269.

104. *Letters*, II:11.

105. Ibid.

106. *Works*, VIII:252.

107. *Works*, VIII:256-257.

108. *Works*, VIII:252-253.

109. D. Michael Henderson, "The Class-Meeting in Methodism and Chartism," an unpublished thesis at Indiana University, Bloomington, Indiana, 1976.

CHAPTER THREE—WESLEY'S SYSTEM OF INTERLOCKING GROUPS

1. Works, VIII:269.

2. George W. Dolbey, *The Architectural Expression of Methodism* (London: The Epworth Press, 1964).

3. *Works*, VII:534.

4. "In the history of Christian doctrine the front rank is rightly reserved for the great speculative theologians-that select company of systematic thinkers who have managed to effect major mutations in the Christian mind. Wesley has no place in this company-nor did he aspire to one. He was, by talent and intent, a folk-theologian: an eclectic who had mastered the secret of plastic synthesis, simple profundity, the common touch. He was an effective evangelist guided by a discriminating theological under-standing, a creative theologian practically involved in the application of his doctrine in the renewal of the church." Outler, *John Wesley*, p. 119.

5. Marshall McLuhan, *Understanding Media: The Extensions of Man* (New York: McGraw Hill, 1964), p. 7ff.

6. Cadman, *Three Religious Leaders of Oxford*, pp. 341-342.

7. For a good treatment of Wesley's evangelical Arminianism, see Bernard Semmel, *The Methodist Revolution* (New York: Basic Books, 1974).

8. John Wesley, *Poetical Works*, I:ix-xxiii.

9. Southey, *Life of Wesley*, II:78.

10. Armstrong, *The Church of England, The Methodists, and Society*, p. 67.

11. Outler, *John Wesley*, pp. 144-146.

12. *Journal*, II:453-454.

13. See McTyeire, *A History of Methodism*, p. 79, and Works, XII:301.

14. Armstrong, *The Church of England*, The Methodists, and Society, p. 67.

15. Wearmouth, *Methodism and the Working-class Movement of England, 1800-1850*.

16. Cadman, *Three Religious Leaders* of Oxford, p. 223.

17. Ibid., pp. 238-239.

18. Richard Niebuhr, *The Social Sources of Denominationalism*, p. 67.

19. Wearmouth, *Methodism and the Working-class Movements of England, 1800-1850*.

20. Davies and Rupp, *A History of the Methodist Church in Great Britain*, p. 310.

21. Ibid.

22. John Wesley, *Poetical Works*, II:17-18.

23. Southey, *Life of Wesley*, II:80-81.

24. Cadman, *Three Religious Leaders of Oxford*, p. 335.

25. For a description of the beginnings, spread, usefulness, evaluation, and objections to the class meeting, see Tyerman, *Life and Times of John Wesley*, I:377-380.

26. Goodell, *The Drillmaster of Methodism*, p. 15.

27. Ibid.

28. See footnote #22, chapter 1 concerning the "Halevy thesis" of Methodism's impact on England.

29. Leslie Church, *The Early Methodist People*, p. 155.

30. *Works*, VIII:252.

31. Ibid., p. 253.

32. *Journal*, II:528.

33. Ibid., II:535.

34. Stevenson, *City Road Chapel*, p. 33.

35. "On God's Vineyard," *Works*, VIII:202-213. See also Outler, *John Wesley*, pp. 104-116.

36. *Works*, VIII:269-270.

37. Ibid.

38. Church, *The Early Methodist People*, p. 168.

39. Church, *More About the Early Methodist People*, pp. 2-3.

40. Miley, *Treatise on the Class-Meeting*, pp. 46-47.

41. Rosser, *Class-Meetings*, p. 162.

42. For more information, see Southey, *Life of Wesley*, II:78.

43. Dr. Jerry Sproull, one of the few contemporary commentators on the class meeting, points out the practicality of the class meeting format in its effect on the Methodist leadership in his thesis, *The Methodist Class-Meeting*, p. 210. See also Fitzgerald, *The Class-Meeting*, pp. 42-43.

44. Church, *The Early Methodist People*, p. 168.

45. Ibid., p. 178.

46. Richard Cameron, *The Rise of Methodism*, p. 300.

47. Davies and Rupp, *A History of the Methodist Church in Great Britain*, I:314.

48. *Poetical Works*, I:326 and I:346.

49. Davies and Rupp, *A History of the Methodist Church in Great Britain*, I:314.

50. Emerick, *Spiritual Renewal*, p. 64.

51. Marshall McLuhan, *The Gutenberg Galaxy*, pp. 137-145.

52. James W. Bashford, *Wesley and Goethe*, pp. 92-93.

53. Quoted in Henry Carter, *The Methodist Heritage*, p. 98.

54. *Works*, VIII:257-258.

55. Benjamin Gregory, *A Handbook of Wesleyan Polity and History*, p. 21.

56. Church, *The Early Methodist People*, pp. 170-171.

57. F. M. Parkinson, "Class Tickets," *Proceedings of the Wesleyan Historical Society*, Vol. 1, Part 5, pp. 129-136.

58. J. G. Wright, "Class and Band Tickets," *Proceedings of the Wesleyan Historical Society*, Vol. V, Part 2, pp. 33-44.

59. Sproull, *The Methodist Class-Meeting*, pp. 73-74.

60. *Works*, III:236.

61. See Schmidt, *John Wesley*, II:i:93.

62. Abel Stevens, *Character-Sketches*, p. 356. Macaulay's full quote was "He [Wesley] was a man whose eloquence and logical acuteness might have made him eminent in literature; whose genius for government was not inferior to that of Richelieu; and who, whatever his errors may have been, devoted all his powers, in defiance of obloquy and derision, to what he considered as the highest good of the species."

63. Ibid., pp. 359-360.

64. Article in *Zion's Herald* (Boston: November 30, 1825), III page 1. It was designated as a reprint from an earlier issue of the Arminian Magazine.

65. Goodell, *The Drillmaster of Methodism*, p. 239.

66. Simon, *John Wesley and the Religious Societies*, p. 9.

67. *Works*, VIII:350-351.

68. "Letter from John Wesley to the Church at Herrnhut, October 14, 1738," *Works*, VI:621.

69. "Letter to Charles Wesley, April 12, 1741," *Journal*, II:448.

70. For a study of Wesley's views on perfection, see Harald Lindstrom, *Wesley and Sanctification*, (Uppsala, Sweden: Almquist and Wiksells Boktryckeri AB, 1947).

71. William James, *Varieties of Religious Experience*, p. 261ff.

72. *Works*, VIII:258-259.

73. Drawn up December 25, 1738. *Works*, VIII:272-273.

74. Ibid.

75. Church, *The Early Methodist People*, p. 151.

76. Ibid.

77. George Stevenson, *City Road Chapel*, p. 39.

78. John Drakeford, "Integrity Therapy," Word Records, Waco, Texas.

79. *Works*, VIII:272-273.

80. Goodell, *The Drillmaster of Methodism*, p. 239.

81. Church, *The Early Methodist People*, pp. 151-152.

82. Southey, *Life of Wesley*, II:372-373.

83. *Works*, VIII:261.

84. Robert Tuttle, *John Wesley: His Life and Theology* (Grand Rapids: Zondervan Publishers, 1958), p. 27.

85. *Works*, VIII:261-262.

86. Simon, *John Wesley and the Methodist Societies*, p. 150.

87. Ibid.

88. Robert Tuttle, *John Wesley*, p. 27. On June 28, 1788, Wesley's eighty-fifth birthday, he was still meeting with a select society.

89. Church, *The Early Methodist People*, pp. 151-152.

90. *Works*, VIII:259-260, "A Plain Account of the People Called Methodists."

91. Ibid.

CHAPTER FOUR—WHY WAS WESLEY'S SYSTEM SO EFFECTIVE?

1. Wesley expressed his esteem for Locke in an essay contained in his *Works*, VIII:455-464. He made several references to the work of Rousseau, like this one in his *Journal* for Saturday, February 3, 1770: "At my leisure moments on several of the following days, I read with much expection a celebrated book,—*Rousseau upon Education*. But how was I disappointed! Sure a more consummate coxcomb never saw the sun! How amazingly

full of himself!... But I object to his temper more than to his judgment; He is a mere misanthrope; a cynic all over.... As to his book, it is whimsical to the last degree; grounded neither upon reason nor experience" (*Works*, III:386-387). On another occasion he referred to Rousseau's *Emilius* as "the most empty, silly, injudicious thing that ever a self-conceited infidel wrote" (*Works*, XIII:474). See also comments in Works, IV:16 and VII:271.

2. Christophers, *The Class-meeting*, pp. 37-38.

3. *Works*, XIII:9.

4. Ibid.

5. See especially Max Weber, *The Protestant Ethic and the Spirit of Capitalism*, tr. Talcott Parsons, (New York: Charles Scribner's Sons, 1958).

6. Christophers, *The Class-meeting*, p. 64.

7. Alfred North Whitehead, *The Aims of Education*, p. 10.

8. Emphasis mine.

9. Matthew 7:24-27.

10. James 1:22.

11. *Works*, VIII:252.

12. *Poetical Works*, I:ix-xxiii.

13. Cell, *Rediscovery of John Wesley*, p. 10.

14. Prince, *John Wesley on Religious Education*, pp. 66-67.

15. See, for example, Peter Wagner's fine treatment of mass movements in *Look Out! The Pentecostals are Coming*.

16. Eric Hoffer, *The True Believer*, pp. 25-26.

17. Norman Mailer, *Armies of the Night* (New York: The New American Library, 1968), pp. 283-284.

18. Niebuhr, *The Social Sources of Denominationalism*, p. 67.

19. Matthew 5:39.

20. Romans 12:21.

21. Ephesians 4:11-12.

22. Hoffer, *The True Believer*, p. 155.

23. Tyerman, *Life and Times of John Wesley*, I:9. Tyerman gives the following statistics of world Methodism, including an estimate of "hearers only": Church members throughout the world 3,063,289; Sunday scholars 3,413,638; Hearers only 6,126,578. Total=12,603,505. This estimate is for the year 1870.

24. Davies and Rupp, *A History of the Methodist Church in Great Britain*, p. 312.

25. See the introduction to Moore's *Pitmen, Preachers, and Politics* (Cambridge: Cambridge University Press, 1974) for a survey of the historiograchical treatments of Methodism.

26. D. D. Thompson, *John Wesley as a Social Reformer*, pp. 103-104.

27. Davies and Rupp, *A History of the Methodist Church in Great Britain*, p. 312.

28. Moore, *Pitmen, Preachers, and Politics*.

29. Davies and Rupp, *A History of the Methodist Church in Great Britain*, p. 312.

30. Tyerman, *Life and Times of John Wesley*, I:10.

31. *Journal*, II:535.

32. See Tyerman, *Life and Times of John Wesley*, I:160-161.

33. Ralph R. Covell and C. Peter Wagner, *An Extension Seminary Primer*, p. 7.

34. Ibid.

35. Christian Lalive d'Epinay, "The Training of Pastors and Theological Education, the Case of Chile," *International Review of Missions* (Geneva: World Council of Churches), Vol. LVI, No. 222, April 1967, pp. 185-192.

36. Stevens, *Character Sketches*, p. 27.

37. Cadman, *Three Religious Leaders of Oxford*, pp. 349-350.

38. Ibid. p. 347.

39. Quoted from *The Gentleman's Magazine*, April 1791, in V. H. H. Green's *John Wesley*, p. 152.

40. Stevens, *Character Sketches*, p. 379-380.